FACTOLOGY

DINOSAURS

& other prehistoric creatures

Open up a world of information!

ARE YOU READY TO EXPLORE...

Forget everything you think you know about dinosaurs and make way for some mind-blowing facts and figures – dinos went extinct 66 million years ago, but their secrets are still being unearthed. There's never been a better time to be obsessed with these strange prehistoric beasts – scientists are using the latest technology to answer our oldest questions: what did dinosaurs really look like? How did they live together? Could they ever walk again?

Leap into a wild world of unimaginable ancient creatures and learn more about the experts doing the digging. From fearsome flyers to frozen forests to giant carnivores, it's time to tear into Earth's most meteoric era yet!

CHAPTER 1
DINOSAUR WORLD

6 Life on Earth
8 Age of the dinosaurs
10 What is a dinosaur?
12 All about evolution
14 Dinosaur family tree
16 Lost worlds
18 Extinction zone
20 What happened to the dinosaurs?

CHAPTER 2
PREHISTORIC SAFARI

26 Awesome ancient animals
32 Something's hatching!
34 Roarsome!
40 Record breakers!
44 Meat-free monsters
50 Fearsome flyers
56 Sea monsters
58 Terror birds
60 Killer crocs
62 Meet the Meg
64 Frozen forests
66 Prehistoric plant life
68 Mega beasts
72 Survivors!
76 The last dinosaurs

CHAPTER 3
DINO SCIENCE

80 What is palaeontology?
82 Prehistoric puzzles
84 Marvellous Mary Anning
88 Rock stars
90 Could dinosaurs walk again?
92 Dinosaurs quiz
94 Glossary & quiz answers
96 Index

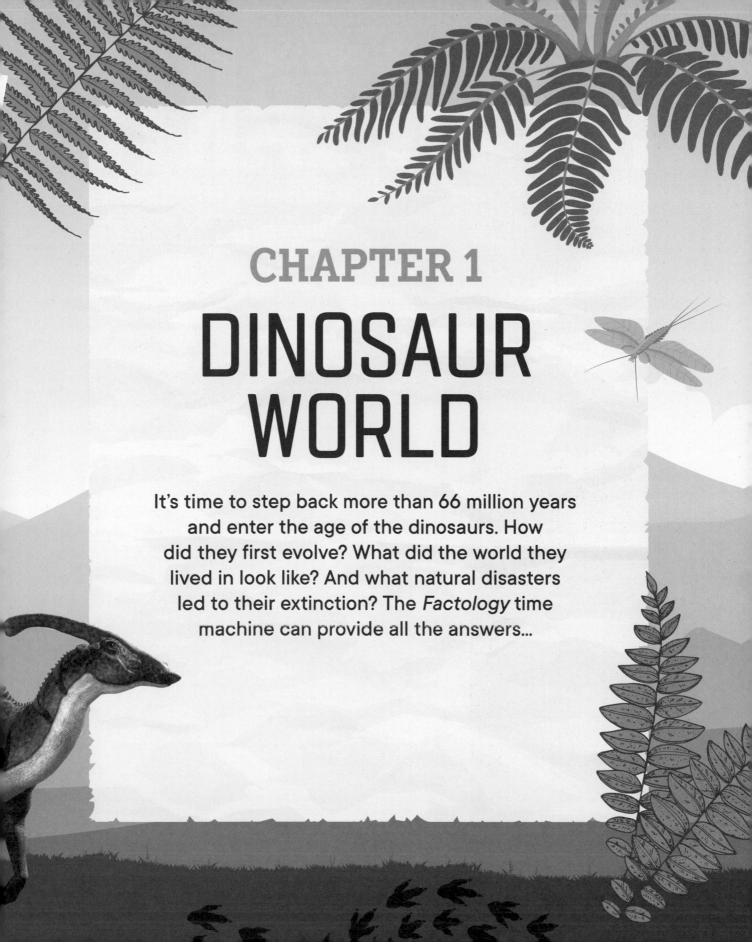

CHAPTER 1

DINOSAUR WORLD

It's time to step back more than 66 million years and enter the age of the dinosaurs. How did they first evolve? What did the world they lived in look like? And what natural disasters led to their extinction? The *Factology* time machine can provide all the answers...

LIFE ON EARTH

More than 4,500,000,000 years ago, the Earth was a lifeless ball of melted rock, covered with burning-hot lava and poisonous gases. As it cooled down over millions of years, a crust formed and rains fell, creating an ocean. Half a billion years or so later, the first forms of life appeared there: tiny microbes multiplied and spread, until some of them began to produce oxygen. Plants started to grow, odd-looking creatures evolved and eventually the first animals crawled out of the sea. Everything alive today shares an ancestry that can be traced back to that time!

TABLE OF TIME

Earth's history is divided into long sections of time called eras, and these are divided into shorter sections called periods. Each period is named after bands of rock in the Earth's crust – together these layers show how and when species evolved, when they thrived and when they went extinct. Let's break down each era...

	ERA	PERIOD	EPOCH
AFTER THE DINOSAURS	CENOZOIC	**Quaternary** *First humans*	Holocene
			Pleistocene
		Neogene *Early primates*	Pliocene
			Miocene
		Paleogene *Rise of mammals*	Oligocene
			Eocene
			Paleocene
AGE OF THE DINOSAURS	MESOZOIC	**Cretaceous**	*First flowers*
		Jurassic	*First birds*
		Triassic	*The rise of dinosaurs*
BEFORE THE DINOSAURS	PALEOZOIC	**Permian**	*First reptiles*
		Carboniferous	*The age of amphibians*
		Devonian	*First seed plants, cartilage fish*
		Silurian	*Earliest land animals*
		Ordovician	*Early bony fish*
		Cambrian	*Invertebrate animals*
	PRE-CAMBRIAN	**Proterozoic**	*First multicellular organisms*
		Archean	*Beginning of the formation of life*
		Hadean	*Formation of the Earth*

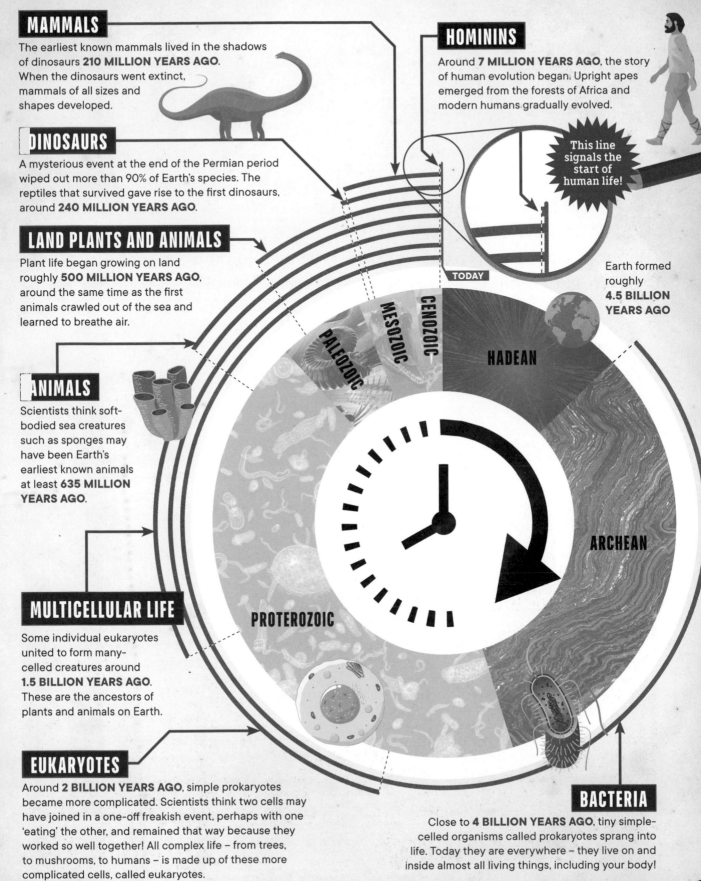

MAMMALS

The earliest known mammals lived in the shadows of dinosaurs **210 MILLION YEARS AGO**. When the dinosaurs went extinct, mammals of all sizes and shapes developed.

DINOSAURS

A mysterious event at the end of the Permian period wiped out more than 90% of Earth's species. The reptiles that survived gave rise to the first dinosaurs, around **240 MILLION YEARS AGO**.

LAND PLANTS AND ANIMALS

Plant life began growing on land roughly **500 MILLION YEARS AGO**, around the same time as the first animals crawled out of the sea and learned to breathe air.

ANIMALS

Scientists think soft-bodied sea creatures such as sponges may have been Earth's earliest known animals at least **635 MILLION YEARS AGO**.

MULTICELLULAR LIFE

Some individual eukaryotes united to form many-celled creatures around **1.5 BILLION YEARS AGO**. These are the ancestors of plants and animals on Earth.

EUKARYOTES

Around **2 BILLION YEARS AGO**, simple prokaryotes became more complicated. Scientists think two cells may have joined in a one-off freakish event, perhaps with one 'eating' the other, and remained that way because they worked so well together! All complex life – from trees, to mushrooms, to humans – is made up of these more complicated cells, called eukaryotes.

HOMININS

Around **7 MILLION YEARS AGO**, the story of human evolution began. Upright apes emerged from the forests of Africa and modern humans gradually evolved.

This line signals the start of human life!

TODAY

Earth formed roughly **4.5 BILLION YEARS AGO**

CENOZOIC

MESOZOIC

PALEOZOIC

HADEAN

ARCHEAN

PROTEROZOIC

BACTERIA

Close to **4 BILLION YEARS AGO**, tiny simple-celled organisms called prokaryotes sprang into life. Today they are everywhere – they live on and inside almost all living things, including your body!

AGE OF THE DINOSAURS

Dinosaurs ruled our planet for around 180 million years during a time called the Mesozoic era. Divided into three parts – the Triassic, the Jurassic and the Cretaceous – this huge age of history saw the Earth change dramatically in climate and landscape, forcing the dinosaurs to evolve and exciting new species to emerge

▲ Coelophysis

START

1 TRIASSIC

252–201 MILLION YEARS AGO

Earth was much hotter than it is today and there was just one dry, desert-like supercontinent called Pangaea, the shape of a giant C.

Reptiles were everywhere! They evolved into the first dinosaurs, which were small and speedy, and the first mammals, which were shrew-like.

Mammal-like reptiles such as Lystrosaurus and small carnivorous dinosaurs like Coelophysis thrived in the Triassic. Ornithosuchus was an ancestor of the crocodile.

Lystrosaurus ▼

The ocean was full of ammonites, fish and big, swimming reptiles like the dolphin-shaped ichthyosaurs.

Pterosaurs, a group of flying reptiles, took to the air during the Triassic.

AT THE END OF THE TRIASSIC PERIOD, SOMETHING CAUSED THE EXTINCTION OF AROUND **80%** OF THE EARTH'S SPECIES!

▲ Ornithosuchus

2 JURASSIC

201-145 MILLION YEARS AGO

This was the golden age of dinosaurs, when warm, humid weather meant plant life flourished and the remarkable reptiles grew to an enormous size! The supercontinent Pangaea split into two, creating Laurasia in the north and Gondwana in the south.

The first bird, **Archaeopteryx**, evolved, and lots of different crocodiles appeared.

Lush plants gave huge herbivores like **Diplodocus** and **Brachiosaurus** plenty to eat.

▲ Diplodocus

Fossils found in Mongolia suggest Jurassic dinos may have been plagued by **giant flea-like insects** around 10 times the size of those you'd find on a dog or cat today, with super painful bites to match!

Fierce hunters like ▲ **Ceratosaurus** preyed on the spiky **Stegosaurus.** ▼

3 CRETACEOUS

145-66 MILLION YEARS AGO

Temperatures dropped further and the first flowers bloomed. Dinosaurs became the most powerful creatures on Earth, while the land beneath them split apart into the continents we know today.

Plant-eaters like **Edmontonia** grew plates and spikes to defend themselves from meat-eaters like the mighty **Tyrannosaurus rex.** ▲

▲ Triceratops

Horned and duck-billed dinosaurs such as **Triceratops** and **Parasaurolophus** thrived.

Two groups of mammals evolved – the marsupials, whose modern descendants include **kangaroos** and **koalas**, and placental mammals, the ancestors of most of today's animals, from **monkeys** to **rats**.

THE PERIOD ENDED WITH A DEVASTATING EXTINCTION EVENT THAT **ALL** NON-BIRD WIPED OUT **ALL** DINOSAURS!

END

WHAT IS A DINOSAUR?

Scientists have been studying these ancient beasts for over 200 years. In that time, a lot of what we know about dinosaurs has changed! Let's bust some myths about dinosaurs...

Most dinosaurs had incredibly strong jaws. Dino skulls had special holes to hold mega muscles. This means even the smallest dinosaurs had a seriously big bite!

GROWTH SPURT

Massive dinos like the super-sized sauropods grew incredibly fast. Fossils show some baby titanosaurs went from the size of a rat to the size of a sheep in just six weeks!

NOT A DINOSAUR

There were lots of other animals living at the same time as the dinos and some of them – such as flying or swimming reptiles – are often wrongly called dinosaurs.

Which of these do you think are dinosaurs?

CROCODILE

PTEROSAUR

ICHTHYOSAUR

ANSWER: NONE OF THE ABOVE!

NEW LOOK

The most famous dinosaur of them all, the Tyrannosaurus rex needs no introduction! Think it looks funny with feathers? Scientists now know that many dinosaurs had feathers on their body. In 2016, the discovery of a 99-million-year-old piece of see-through amber showed a feathered dino tail, proving that two-legged theropods like the T-rex had fluffy feathers!

WALKING TALL

You might think any animal living before humans walked the Earth counted as a dinosaur, but that's not true. Today, if a prehistoric beast ticks these boxes, most scientists will agree that it counts as a dinosaur:

✓ IT LIVED 230-66 MILLION YEARS AGO

✓ IT LIVED ON LAND

✓ IT LAID EGGS

✓ MOST IMPORTANTLY, IT WALKED UPRIGHT WITH ITS LIMBS UNDERNEATH ITS BODY, RATHER THAN SPREAD OUT TO THE SIDE LIKE A LIZARD OR CROCODILE.

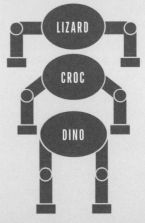

LIZARD

CROC

DINO

SIZE MATTERS

Not all dinosaurs were as big as you might imagine. Scientists think so many larger dinosaur bones have been discovered because they were more likely to fossilise over time. In reality, dinos ranged in size from tiny ones like Anchiornis (just 40cm long!) to the gigantic sauropods, which could grow longer than a tennis court!

40CM

ALL ABOUT
EVOLUTION

Why did some dinosaurs develop long necks, while others were packed with plates and spikes? Because life on Earth is constantly in the process of changing...

WHO WILL SURVIVE?

Fossils reveal the incredible truth that animals didn't suddenly appear on the planet the way they are now – life on Earth has evolved over millions of years. As early species adapted to survive in their environment, new ones developed. That's because of a process called **natural selection**. Here's how it works...

1 Animals and plants produce lots of offspring, and none of them are exactly the same. Two siblings might look alike, but there are subtle variations. Maybe one can jump higher, while another has better eyesight.

2 Thanks to genetics, these variations can be passed from parents to their offspring. Do you share any traits with a parent?

3 Have you ever heard the phrase 'survival of the fittest'? The idea is that those offspring born with variations that help them survive (like armoured plates which protect them from predators) will be the ones to have more offspring.

4 Surviving offspring keep passing on their variations until, in time, those helpful variations may become a trait of that species. Sometimes a lifeform changes so much, it becomes a whole new species!

A WHALE'S JOURNEY

Fifteen years ago, fossil hunters found the remains of the whale's earliest ancestor – and it looked like a cat-sized deer! Scientists think it took 10 million years for these land mammals to evolve into today's whales, dolphins and porpoises...

GLORIOUS GROUPS

Scientists look at the similarities and differences between animals and try to group them together according to the features they share. Dinosaurs, for example, are part of a group called vertebrates – *animals with a backbone*. Humans are part of that group too.

Vertebrates can be divided again into smaller groups with similar traits – fish, amphibians, reptiles, birds and mammals.

Dinosaurs are reptiles and they share certain traits that set them apart from other groups. It's these features that help scientists to recognise a dino fossil when it's unearthed.

VERTEBRATES
ANIMALS WITH BACKBONE

Fish backbone

AMPHIBIAN

Have smooth, moist skin (no scales). Breathe with gills and lungs

Cold-blooded

Spend part of their lives in water and part on land, and lay eggs

BIRD

Have feathers, a beak and wings

Warm-blooded

Their babies hatch from eggs

FISH

Have gills to breathe, scales and fins on their bodies

Cold-blooded

Live in water

MAMMAL

Have hair or fur

Warm-blooded

Drink milk when they are babies

REPTILE

Have scales and breathe with lungs

Cold-blooded

Usually lay eggs on land

CHANGING WORLD

The ideas that scientists have about dinosaurs also change and evolve with time – and they don't always get it right! The Velociraptor is the perfect example. If the movies are to be believed, these were scaly, people-sized predators. Yet fossil evidence has shown them to be far smaller – the size of a goose – and covered in feathers!

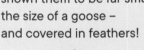

THEN

NOW

NAME GAME

In 1842, famously grumpy scientist Richard Owen mashed together the ancient Greek words for '*terrible*' and '*lizard*' and came up with the word '*dinosaur*'. He was the first to realise that fascinating fossils being uncovered at the time had certain unique similarities and needed their own animal group name – 'dinosauria'.

DEINOS (TERRIBLE) + SAUROS (LIZARD) = DINOSAURIA

DINOSAUR FAMILY TREE

How dinosaurs evolved is a question that scientists are still trying to answer! Looking at fossils, experts agree that crocodiles, dinosaurs and birds all had a common ancestor – the archosaur – and that dinos first appeared around 240 million years ago. Which groups go together isn't always clear cut, but this family tree gives you a good idea of how different dinosaurs evolved...

CROCODILIANS

Today's crocodiles, alligators and gharials all descended from archosaurs.

CERATOPSIANS

These four-legged plant-eaters had parrot-like beaks and huge heads adorned with horns and frills.

ARCHOSAURS

Dinosaurs, birds and crocodiles all evolved from a larger group of 'ruling reptiles' called the archosaurs.

PTEROSAURS

These flying reptiles ranged in size from a sparrow to twice the size of an ostrich!

DINOSAUROMORPHS

These small reptiles were the early relatives of dinosaurs.

ORNITHOSCELIDANS

Some scientists recently shook up the dino family tree by adding theropods and ornithiscians to this new group.

DINOSAURS

In the early Triassic period dinos appeared and began to diversify into lots of different groups.

SAUROPODOMORPHS

These gentle giants developed long necks and tails and many never stopped growing.

STEGOSAURS & ANKYLOSAURS

These armoured beasts boasted fearsome spikes and bony plates.

HADROSAURS

Often called duck-billed dinosaurs because of their funny-shaped beaks, they had complex plant-munching teeth.

OTHER THEROPODS

Tyrannosaurus rex was one of the largest ever meat-eaters, rocking 60 or so carrot-sized teeth!

THEROPODS

Mostly meat-eaters, this diverse group of dinos gave rise to the birds we know today.

BIRDS

Achaeopteryx, the earliest known bird, had characteristics of both birds (feathered wings) and reptiles (a bony tail).

LOST WORLDS

Many millions of years ago at the time when dinosaurs first appeared, the land beneath their feet was very different than it is today. Why is that?

ONE AND ONLY

Earth has gone through plenty of changes during its 4.5 billion year history. For one thing, it hasn't always had seven continents – at one point they were all joined up! About 300 million years ago, one third of our planet's surface was arranged into a supercontinent called Pangaea ('all earth' in Greek), while the rest was a single ocean: Panthalassa ('all sea'). Geography class would've been easier in those days! This was the world where the dinosaurs first evolved until, around 200 million years ago, Pangaea began to break apart – first into two giant land masses (Gondwana in the south and Laurasia in the north), then into the modern continents as we know them.

NORTH AND SOUTH

Pangaea was huge – covering about 30% of the Earth's surface! – and with its mostly hot, dry climate, there was little biodiversity. As fragmentation and climate change followed, the southern dinosaurs began evolving independently from the northern dinosaurs, and like any species adapting to new environments, this led to a great variety of plant and animal life.

PANGAEA
Permian – 250 million years ago

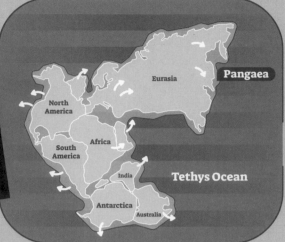

LAURASIA & GONDWANA
Triassic – 200 million years ago

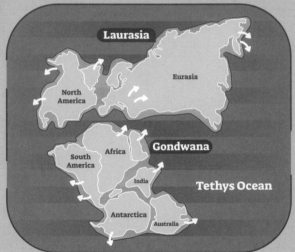

PRESENT
Quaternary

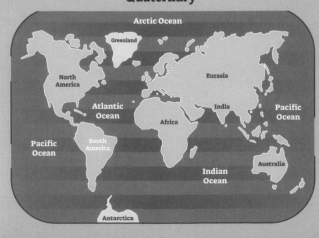

AHEAD OF HIS TIME

It was German meteorologist Alfred Wegener who first proposed the idea in 1912 that the continents had once been fused together in a supercontinent, and then gradually drifted apart. As well as showing how continental borders could be matched up, he presented evidence of similar plant and animal fossils and rocks of the same age found on continents now far apart. But his 'continental drift' theory was ridiculed by the scientific community! Sadly his idea of the Earth's crust being broken into pieces like a jigsaw puzzle wasn't formally recognised until many decades later, in the mid-20th century.

PLANETARY PUZZLE

Look closely at a world map: can you see how the east coast of South America fits almost perfectly into the west coast of Africa? Now look at the outline of the other continents on a map and try to work out where they could have once connected!

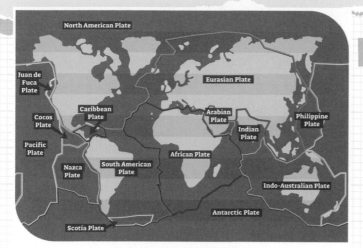

POWERFUL PLATES

Continents shift around the globe just a few centimetres a year – about as fast as your fingernails grow! – thanks to huge slabs of rocks called tectonic plates that make up the Earth's outer shell. Fifteen of these plates float on the surface and fit nicely into one another – most of the time. As they follow currents deep inside the Earth they can move in different directions, causing them to collide, pull apart or slide past one another, triggering destructive earthquakes and tsunamis. When they meet and push together, they can also create beautiful landscapes – from majestic volcanoes to spectacular mountains.

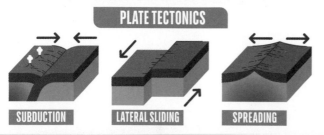

PLATE TECTONICS

SUBDUCTION LATERAL SLIDING SPREADING

A HOLE NEW WORLD

Geologists have noticed that supercontinents form and break up about every 500 million years – it seems like our continents are starting to come together again! Pangaea may be (very) slowly reassembling, but don't worry, Pangaea version 2 isn't due for another 250 million years! Geologists can roughly work out the positions of the continents based on trajectories of the current plate movements, even though it's still too early to predict. One plausible scenario, called Pangaea Ultima, pictures a doughnut-shaped landmass with the remnant of an ocean in the middle. One thing's for sure: we won't be around to see this new ring-shaped world!

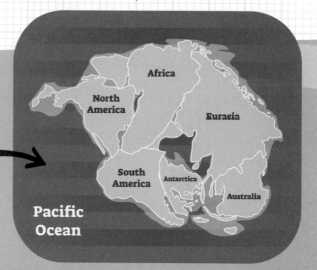

ANCIENT SUPERCONTINENTS

Proving Pangaea existed was one thing, but geology (the study of rocks in the Earth's crust) has since revealed that other supercontinents preceded it! The very first was Vaalbara, which formed over three BILLION years ago!

EXTINCTION ZONE

Over Earth's amazing 4.5 billion-year history, there have been five mass extinctions – major disasters when whole groups of plants and animals disappeared completely. Each event is named after the geological period it occurred in, or the periods just before or after it happened. Scientists think they know what caused some of the mass extinctions, but others remain a total mystery...

DISAPPEARING ACT

When a species of animal or plant disappears, scientists say it's become extinct. It's natural for a certain number of species to die out over time as it helps drive the evolution of life. When animals and plants go extinct, their role in the planet's ecosystem usually gets filled by new species or ones that already exist. Since the beginning of life on Earth, there have been mass extinction events that have wiped out huge numbers of species.

EXTINCT

Last seen in 1662, the dodo was sadly hunted to extinction by humans

EXTINCT

Billions of passenger pigeons once flew over North America, but over-hunting caused these beautiful birds to die out in 1914

EXTINCT

The last known Tasmanian tiger died in 1936. Found in Australia, Tasmania and New Guinea, hunting and habitat destruction were among the reasons this marsupial became extinct

IT'S THOUGHT THAT **99% OF ALL ORGANISMS** THAT HAVE EVER EXISTED ON EARTH **HAVE GONE EXTINCT**

1 ORDOVICIAN-SILURIAN EXTINCTION

443 MILLION YEARS AGO

The world's first ever mass extinction happened 443 million years ago. Scientists think global cooling – which made huge glaciers form and sea levels drop – caused 85% of all species, which were mostly marine organisms, to die out.

2 DEVONIAN EXTINCTION

374 MILLION YEARS AGO

It's not known what triggered the planet's second mass extinction but scientists believe environmental changes played a part in it. The Devonian mass extinction happened 374 million years ago, and eliminated about 75% of the world's species.

Fossils, such as these fossilised Scaphites, help scientists understand why species have gone extinct throughout history ▶

3 PERMIAN-TRIASSIC EXTINCTION

252 MILLION YEARS AGO

Earth's third mass extinction, known as the Permian-Triassic, happened around 252 million years ago, and killed off a whopping 90% of all Earth's creatures! It's thought volcanic eruptions and an asteroid were probably the cause.

The death of the Dimetrodon in the Permian-Triassic extinction made room for new creatures, including the first dinosaurs.

4 TRIASSIC-JURASSIC EXTINCTION

201 MILLION YEARS AGO

Earth's fourth mass extinction event took place 201 million years ago. Scientists think climate change, volcanic activity and rising sea levels caused the Triassic-Jurassic extinction, which wiped out around 80% of life on Earth, including many types of dinosaurs.

5 CRETACEOUS EXTINCTION

66 MILLION YEARS AGO

The fifth mass extinction happened 66 million years ago when a gigantic asteroid or comet crashed into Earth, killing off the dinosaurs.

WHY DOES EXTINCTION HAPPEN?

Extinction is driven by environmental changes and evolutionary challenges. Changing habitats and difficulties reproducing are among the reasons a species might disappear. Human activities can cause animals and plants to die out too.

A NEW MASS EXTINCTION?

Scientists believe Earth could be going through a sixth mass extinction – and it's one caused by humans. It's thought that pollution, habitat destruction and climate change could see 50% of the planet's species extinct by 2100. So how do we stop it? Research shows that if we change how people use natural resources, Earth's future could be much brighter. Are there any climate change issues affecting your local community that you could explore and get involved with?

EXTINCT

Discovered in 1964, the golden toad died out in 1989. It was the first known species to become extinct because of climate change ▶

DINOSAURS RULED THE EARTH FOR MORE THAN

180 MILLION YEARS

THERE WERE AT LEAST A

THOUSAND SPECIES

OF THESE IMPRESSIVE BEASTS

THEY LIVED ON EVERY CONTINENT

INCLUDING ANTARCTICA

BUT 66 MILLION YEARS AGO
DINOSAURS SUDDENLY
DIED OUT

WHAT HAPPENED TO THE DINOSAURS?

A catastrophic event at the end of the Cretaceous period caused one of the most dramatic mass extinctions that Earth has ever seen. Read on to find out what finished off these mega monsters...

COLLISION COURSE

So how did the largest animals ever to live on land become extinct? Most scientists think dinosaurs were killed off when a giant asteroid or comet – known as the Chicxulub Impactor – smashed into the Earth. Chicxulub was so big, it created an enormous crater off the coast of Mexico's Yucatan Peninsula, measuring 150km (93 miles) across and 20km (12 miles) deep.

Recent research suggests Chicxulub came from a shell of icy debris found at the edge of the solar system, known as the Oort cloud

DANGEROUS FALLOUT

The Chicxulub's impact is thought to have created a giant 1.5km-high tsunami (a series of seriously massive waves) that wreaked havoc on the Earth's oceans, triggering earthquakes and volcanic eruptions all over the world. The crash also created a shockwave and a powerful air blast – with winds of over 1,000km/h near the impact site – sending huge amounts of hot rock into the atmosphere, which started forest fires and destroyed everything in its path.

NO MORE SUN

The massive impact also blasted particles and gas into the atmosphere, which blocked out a lot of the Sun's rays for decades, acidified the oceans, and plunged the planet into a lengthy winter. This sudden change affected all creatures, made living conditions much harsher and caused the extinction of around three-quarters of all plant and animal life on Earth.

THE LACK OF SUNLIGHT MEANT EARTH'S SURFACE TEMPERATURE DROPPED BY UP TO 28°C!

CLIMATE CATASTROPHE?

Some scientists think global warming was involved in the extinction of dinosaurs. With the Earth's climate changing over millions of years and large volcanic eruptions that lasted tens of thousands of years – creating large-scale climate change – it's thought the planet may have gradually become uninhabitable for dinosaurs.

Other scientists think it was a combination of the Chicxulub Impactor and ongoing climate change. What do you think caused the extinction?

THE MASS EXTINCTION ENDED THE AGE OF THE DINOSAURS, BUT IT ALSO LEFT GAPS IN THE WORLD'S ECOSYSTEMS, WHICH WERE FILLED BY BIRDS – THE ONLY DINOSAURS TO SURVIVE – AND MAMMALS. THE ANIMALS THAT SURVIVED WENT ON TO EVOLVE INTO THE CREATURES THAT LIVE ON EARTH NOW... INCLUDING US!

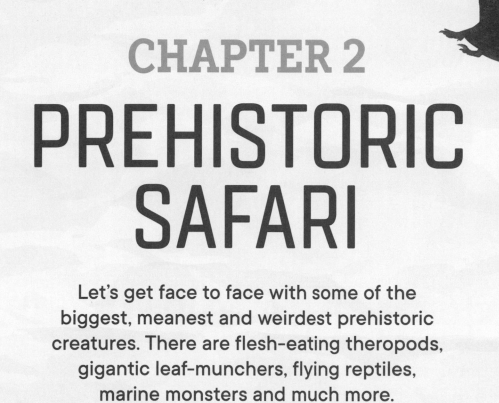

CHAPTER 2
PREHISTORIC SAFARI

Let's get face to face with some of the biggest, meanest and weirdest prehistoric creatures. There are flesh-eating theropods, gigantic leaf-munchers, flying reptiles, marine monsters and much more.
How big were dinosaur eggs? What dinosaur had the longest tail? And which dinosaurs survived to the present day?
It's time to find out...

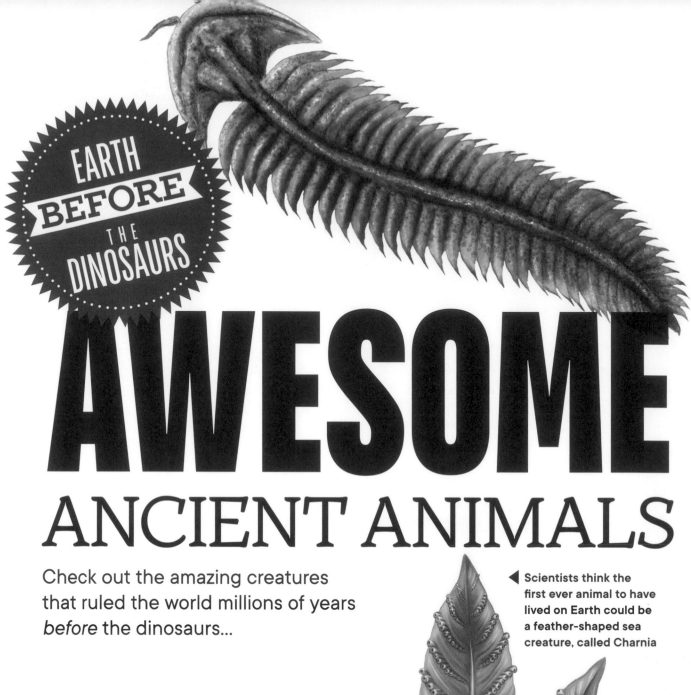

AWESOME
ANCIENT ANIMALS

Check out the amazing creatures
that ruled the world millions of years
before the dinosaurs...

◀ Scientists think the
first ever animal to have
lived on Earth could be
a feather-shaped sea
creature, called Charnia

1 EARLY LIFE

The world's first animals were sea creatures – they had
no head, limbs or sense organs. These early animals
lived in the Precambrian era on ancient sea beds,
where their soft disc or leaf-shaped bodies
gathered food from the water.

27

SPIDERS THE SIZE OF **SMALL DOGS**

2 CARBONIFEROUS CRITTERS

Around 360 million years ago, during the Carboniferous period, Earth was covered in hot, humid swamps and rainforests. These dense, swampy forests were home to all sorts of strange creatures, including gigantic poisonous centipedes, huge one-metre-long cockroaches and scorpions, spiders the size of small dogs, and dragonflies that grew to the size of *seagulls*!

360 MILLION YEARS AGO

▶ At over 5 metres long and 2 metres wide, Arthropleura is thought to be the largest land-dwelling bug of all time!

5 METRE LONG BUG

3 RETRO REPTILES

Over time Earth became hotter and drier and during the Permian period (299 million years ago) prehistoric fish and sharks swam in the oceans while amphibians and insects, along with early reptiles – known as synapsids – dominated the land. Synapsids looked like crocodiles and even dinosaurs and had sail fans, sabre-fangs and odd-shaped skulls.

▲ The sail-backed Edaphosaurus's large back fin was used to regulate its body temperature

◀ The sabre-fanged carnivore Inostrancevia was a fearsome predator

299 MILLION YEARS AGO

Varanops were 1.5 metres long and mostly chomped on insects ▶

◄ The Dimetrodon was a meat-eating predator that moved like a crocodile

▼ Estemmenosuchus used bony knots on its skull to protect itself from predators

4 ANCIENT RELATIVES

LASTED 47 MILLION YEARS

The Permian period lasted around 47 million years and towards the end of it a population of synapsids had evolved into early mammals. From apex predators like the Dimetrodon to plant-eating herbivores like Estemmenosuchus, these protomammals were our ancient relatives, and they thrived on land until a massive event changed the course of life on Earth forever...

5 MASS EXTINCTION

Around 252 million years ago, the biggest mass extinction in Earth's history marked the end of the Permian period. The event wiped out 70% of land animals and 95% of sea life on Earth. No one knows for sure what caused the mass extinction but it's thought a huge asteroid crashing into Earth at the same time as a series of volcanic eruptions is to blame.

252 MILLION YEARS AGO

6 RISE OF THE DINOSAURS

After the mass extinction opened up Earth's ecosystems, the Triassic period (252-201 million years ago) saw new kinds of terrestrial and marine creatures evolve, including lizard-like reptiles known as archosaurs. It took more than 30 million years, but dinosaurs slowly evolved from a group of these archosaurs known as dinosauromorphs. These primitive reptiles didn't look like T-rex or Stegosaurus though – they had long limbs, walked on all fours and were the same size as a pet cat today!

▲ The Lagerpeton was a small dinosauromorph that used quick reflexes and speed to avoid predators

◄ The Silesaurus had a distinctive beaked jaw and bird-like skull

DID YOU know?

Crocodiles and alligators are living archosaurs that descended from ancient reptile relatives.

SOMETHING'S HATCHING!

Do you think a dinosaur could be cute? All creatures must come from somewhere, and all dinosaurs hatched from eggs. How hard is an ancient eggshell? And what did baby theropods eat? Let's crack on...

BIG BABIES

Modern research proves that lots of dinosaur species had feathers lining their scaly skin, so it's likely that baby dinosaurs looked a lot like ducklings. Cute! A baby Tyrannosaurus rex, for instance, was fuzzy... and the size of a small turkey. The bigger the dinosaur, the bigger the egg – the Diplodocus laid eggs the size of a grapefruit. Ouch!

IT TOOK THE TYRANNOSAURUS REX

AROUND 17 YEARS

TO REACH ITS FULL ADULT SIZE

CIRCLE OF LIFE

By now, you know that dinosaurs can be seriously heavy. Yet even though some dinosaur eggs were tougher than bird eggs, they could still be cracked – that's why you'll see their eggs laid out in circles. Oviraptorids and similar species would carefully lay their eggs with enough space to sit in the middle of the mound. This meant it could cover the eggs without damaging its babies, and keep them warm and safe from predators.

Eggs-traordinary!

Not a single species of dinosaur egg was bigger than 60cm – not even a titanosaur's. Some scientists now think that early dinosaurs had soft eggs, like turtles.

SMALL SCIENCE

The first ever dinosaur fossil found in Italy was this baby Scipionyx – it may have been only three weeks old when it started to fossilise 113 million years ago. Scientists have been stunned at just how well preserved its internal organs are and its stomach even shows that 'Ciro' (a common name for Italian boys) had wolfed down tiny reptiles and fish. Which tiny dino would you like to find a fossil of?

DIFFERENT DIETS

Humans need a balanced diet to grow up big and strong... and it looks like dinosaurs did too. Palaeontologists have discovered young dinos that had teeth when their parents didn't. One explanation for this is that even herbivorous theropods like the little Limusaurus needed the protein boost from meat to make it past their early years and adapt. It went veggie later.

THE LONGEST NAME FOR A DINOSAUR IS
MICROPACHYCEPHALOSAURUS
– A TINY THICK-HEADED LIZARD

PROTECT YOUR NEST

Today, mammal species like lions, orangutans and polar bears are fiercely protective of their young, and scientists say some dinosaur species were too. The oldest dinosaur eggs in existence belonged to the Maiasaura, which means 'good mother lizard'. These late Cretaceous herbivores nested together in large groups – there's strength in numbers.

ROARSOME!

These carnivorous hunters are the deadliest creatures that ever lived. Fuelled by hunger, these remarkable reptiles used sharp teeth, strong legs and quick reflexes to eliminate their prey. Just be glad they're not around today!

3X HEAVIER THAN T-REX

SPINOSAURUS

DANGER 10 RATING

Get out of the water! The largest known carnivorous dinosaur used its webbed claws and long tail to turn any stretch of water into its hunting grounds. Its long, narrow, crocodile-like nose was perfect for silently stalking fish and smaller prey.

This aquatic hunter wasn't as quick on dry land, but scientists think it used its straight, spiny teeth to spear victims and shake them until pieces tore off. It's now thought the sail on its back wasn't to keep it cool – but the ultimate status symbol. Don't mess with this dino.

DATA

NAME *Spīna* (thorny) + *sauros* (lizard)

LIVED 100-94 million years ago – the Cretaceous period

SIZE 7 metres high, 18 metres long – the length of a bowling lane

WEIGHT 13-22 tons – three times as heavy as a T-rex

KILLER EDGE Its perfect water-based design

FACT A SPINOSAURUS FOSSIL WAS BLOWN UP DURING WORLD WAR II, PUSHING RESEARCH ABOUT IT BACK BY DECADES.

TYRANNOSAURUS REX

Meet the most famously ferocious dinosaur of them all. The king of dinosaurs might have only had short, scrappy arms, but it used its super-charged senses to sniff out prey... and even other hunters' lunch.

The T-rex stalked the forests of what is now western America, and its powerful jaws meant it only needed to clamp down ONCE to tear through each victim. It's one of the dinos most closely related to birds today – but you wouldn't guess that from its teeth. As we know from the movies, if you see a T-rex... run!

DATA

NAME *Turanno* (tyrant) + *sauros* (lizard) + *rex* (king)

LIVED 68-66 million years ago – the very end of the Cretaceous period

SIZE 6 metres high, 12 metres long – that's as tall as a giraffe

WEIGHT 7 tons – the same as an African elephant

KILLER EDGE Its 60 saw-edged teeth

DANGER **9** RATING

SAME HEIGHT

FACT A TYRANNOSAURUS REX NEEDED TO EAT THE SAME AMOUNT EACH DAY AS 80 PEOPLE. IT COULD TEAR OFF 200KG OF FLESH IN A SINGLE BITE... THAT WOULD BE A PRETTY BIG BURGER.

TWO-LEGGED TERROR

Dinosaurs like tyrannosaurs were called Theropoda, which literally means 'beast feet'. It's a perfect way to describe just how good these two-legged tyrants were at closing the gap. Imagine a race between an ostrich and a cow and you'll get an idea of how hardy herbivores needed to be.

MEAT-EATERS

HERBIVORES

EAT UP

Carnivorous dinosaurs only made up 35% of all dinosaurs. Why? If meat-eaters multiplied too quickly, there wouldn't be enough plant eaters to go around. This delicate balance of life is called an 'equilibrium'.

DANGER 8 RATING

VELOCIRAPTOR

Super fast and super smart, Velociraptors knew how to take care of their prey effectively. Sprinting through the undergrowth, they were masters of staying silent... and violent. Moving faster than a tiger, the Velociraptor made sure its prey had no idea it was being hunted.

Today, scientists think they were more bird-like than ever. They evolved to be land-based, and could scavenge the remains of much bigger hunters' meals. The 'fast thief' would leap towards its targets using the huge, rounded claws on its back feet to take them down instantly. These tiny nightmares would have been a big threat for slower-moving dinos.

DATA

NAME *Velox* (fast) + *raptor* (thief)

LIVED 80-69 million years ago – late Cretaceous period

SIZE 0.5 metres high, 1.8 metres long – about the same size as a wolf

WEIGHT 25kg – roughly the same as a beaver

KILLER EDGE The hooked claws on its hind legs... they could tear through pretty much anything!

WOLF-SIZE

2X HEAVIER THAN T-REX

GIGANOTOSAURUS

A taller, leaner hunter than the Tyrannosaurus rex, the Giganotosaurus used its serrated teeth to slice through targets and, unlike other predators, probably relied on multiple bites to bring them down.

Only discovered in 1993, the Giganotosaurus changed the way we see dinosaurs beyond the films. Active in the swamplands of what would become South America, it had a brain the shape and size of a banana and mainly focused on slow-moving herbivores... dinosaurs with plenty of flesh to chew on. It's possible these huge predators also hunted in packs – which would have made them a GIANT menace.

DATA

NAME *Gigās* (giant) + *notos* (south) + *sauros* (lizard)

LIVED 97-96 million years ago – the early Cretaceous period

SIZE 13 metres long – one and a half London buses

WEIGHT 14 tons – that's TWO tyrannosaurs

KILLER EDGE Its 76 knife-like, 8-inch teeth

FACT EVEN ITS HEAD WAS BIGGER THAN A FULLY-GROWN HUMAN!

DANGER 10 RATING

UTAHRAPTOR

Three times bigger than the Velociraptor, the Utahraptor is the ultimate carnivorous killing machine. Using 30 rounded claws the same length as a T-rex's teeth, it would bludgeon future meals with its feet, claws and jaws. Its leg bones were super thick to make sure it could keep on kicking killing blows.

The largest raptor so far discovered, it was almost certainly warm-blooded – a fast metabolism (how fast a body changes food into energy) would have let it hunt longer and move quicker than ANY of the plant-eating prey it hunted. What a horror!

DATA

NAME *Utah* (in America) + *raptor* (thief)

LIVED 125 million years ago – early Cretaceous period

SIZE 6 metres – one and half Volkswagen Beetles long

WEIGHT Up to 1 ton – the same weight as a walrus

KILLER EDGE Its shock-absorbing, stabbing back legs. The Utahraptor had deadly feet

DEADLY FEET

CARNOTAURUS

It's time to MEAT your new favourite dinosaur! The Carnotaurus sastrei stalked South America, laying waste to smaller dinosaurs with its battering ram horns and fearsome jaws. With a name that translates as the 'meat-eating bull', it's one of only two dinosaurs named after a modern mammal. This hungry menace had even shorter arms than the T-rex – were they used for balance, or would another few million years of evolution have seen them disappear?

Only one Carnotaurus has been found, but it was in such good condition that we've learned a lot about this Cretaceous killer. Due to the size of other dinosaurs in Patagonia, we know the Carnotaurus would have been an apex predator... the most dangerous hunter around.

DATA

NAME Carne (meat-eating) + taurus (bull)

LIVED 72-69 million years ago – late Cretaceous period

SIZE 9 metres – nearly as tall as a Brachiosaurus

WEIGHT Two tons – the same as a Jeep Cherokee

KILLER EDGE A horned head blow from the Carnotaurus would be deadly to smaller creatures

FACT DON'T LIKE THE IDEA OF DINOSAURS BEING COVERED IN FEATHERS? NEW RESEARCH SHOWS THAT THE CARNOTAURUS HAD SUPER SCALES THAT HELPED IT KEEP COOL AT ALL TIMES.

BIRDS OF A FEATHER

So what else links two-legged therapods to their bird-shaped brethren today? All therapods had three-toed feet (great for keeping your balance) and a wishbone... just like the one your family might crack open during a roast chicken dinner. They also had hollow bones, which made them lighter.

RECORD BREAKERS!

To thrive and survive in the Mesozoic era, you had to stand out from the crowd. Let's get up close and personal with some wicked reptilian record breakers...

ALMOST ACTUAL-SIZE TOOTH

THE DINO WITH THE SHORTEST NAME IS

THE YI

IT'S A SCANSORIOPTERYGID

FROM JURASSIC CHINA

BIGGEST TEETH →

The famously ferocious **TYRANNOSAURUS REX** needed long teeth to make short work of its prey. That's why it had 60 teeth to tear up food and each one was the same length as a shatter-proof ruler. Imagine a dinosaur's dentist bill!

THE T-REX'S
30CM TEETH
WERE TERRIFYING

← SMARTEST

The **TROODON** might not have had the biggest brain (that's the Tyrannosaurus rex!), but it was certainly the smartest. The Troodon formosus had agile arms and incredible vision – and could plan how it was going to use them *before* the hunt.

THE BIGGEST DINOSAUR POOS CAME FROM THE

ARGENTINOSAURUS

SCIENTISTS THINK THEY COULD HAVE BEEN 400KG

THAT'S 1,000 TIMES BIGGER THAN A HUMAN'S!

400KG

↙ SMILIEST

Feeling hungry? Roaming what is modern Niger's Sahara Desert, the **NIGERSAURUS** needed all of its 500 pearly whites to break down plant-based foods close to the ground. Its massive muzzle helped it get up close and personal with the lushest of plants. Open wide!

↓ BIGGEST

Today, the blue whale is the biggest creature around. Rewind to the Mesozoic era and the long-necked sauropods were head and shoulders above the rest. The **DREADNOUGHTUS** was a towering 26 metres – taller than four giraffes.

↑ FASTEST

Ready, set, go! Manchester University recently calculated the running speeds of a prehistoric line-up to see which dinosaur truly was fastest. At 65km/h, the pint-sized **COMPSOGNATHUS** could keep up with a hare today – and easily outrun a human. Winner!

↓ SMALLEST

Get your magnifying glass out. Staying small is a fantastic mode of camouflage and the mini **MICRORAPTOR ZHAOIANUS** was the tiniest dinosaur at just 39cm – the same size as a chicken. Being small made flying a breeze, and it didn't need to eat as much food.

→ LONGEST TAIL

The **DIPLODOCUS** didn't just have a long neck... it had a long tail to balance it out! At a whopping 14 metres, that's the longest rudder of any animal, dead or alive. It's about as long as the Hollywood sign – no wonder they put it in *Jurassic Park*!

→ MOST RECENT

The **CHENANISAURUS BARBARICUS** was the last lizard standing. Discovered in Morocco, this two-legged terror reigned at the very end of the Cretaceous period. Just 66 million years ago, it would have seen the first-ever flowering plants emerge.

THE DIMMEST DINOSAUR WAS THE

STEGOSAURUS

SCIENTISTS USED TO THINK

ITS BRAIN WAS IN ITS BACKSIDE!

↑ BEST SWIMMER

Dinosaurs might have been land-based, but that didn't stop them from swimming. Evidence suggests that the towering **SPINOSAURUS** not only used its dolphin-like fins to hunt fish, but it probably loved wallowing in swamps, too.

MEAT-FREE MONSTERS

Don't forget to eat your greens! If you weren't eating meat in the Mesozoic era, chances are you were a herbivore. These veggie-chomping giants had to eat HUGE amounts of plant life to stay energised. Most herbivorous dinosaurs had teeth ready to tear up the toughest roots and barks, and you wouldn't want to pick a fight with one. These stubborn beasts had deadly defences...

THAGOMIZER

STEGOSAURUS

DEFENCE RATING 8

One of the most instantly recognisable four-legged dinosaurs, the Stegosaurus has been hotly debated by scientists. Why did that row of upright plates on its back (some of which were more than a metre long) ever evolve?

With its strangely small head (housing a brain the shape and size of a bent hot dog), it's also unknown how hard the Stegosaurus could bite with its beak. One thing we can be sure of, however, is its main defence tactic: swinging its spiky tail like a medieval mace! And it was efficient at processing food – less waste means more haste when a Tyrannosaurus rex is on your tail.

DATA

NAME *Stegē* (roof) + *sauros* (lizard)

LIVED 150-145 million years ago – the late Jurassic/early Cretaceous period

SIZE Up to 9 metres – that's almost as long as a telephone pole is tall

WEIGHT Up to 7 tons – about the same as an elephant

BEST DEFENCE The Stegosaurus's thagomizer. That's the name for its tail branch of death!

HEAVY AS AN ELEPHANT

800
VEGGIE
MUNCHING
TEETH

DEFENCE RATING
9

AS LONG AS A BUS

TRICERATOPS

This iconic dinosaur was certainly no meat-eater. Unlike the huge jaws of most carnivores, its bird-like beak helped it grab hold of shrubs and ferns and turn them into food. With a mouth full of 800 incredible teeth that were always regrowing, it could slice and chew through the thickest roots. No veggie was too tough.

Making its home in modern America and Canada, it could hold its own thanks to three super sharp face spikes. Using a mix of its horns and weight to defend itself from predators, the Triceratops moved in herds like the grazers of today to stay safe. This species of ceratopsian was certainly no pushover.

DATA

NAME *Trikeratos* (three-horned) + *ōps* (face)

LIVED 88-66 million years ago – late Cretaceous period

SIZE 9 metres – about the same length as a bus

WEIGHT 8 tons – the same as two hippopotamuses

BEST DEFENCE Its three fierce face horns

FACT A TRICERATOPS' TEETH GREW IN WHAT ARE CALLED BATTERIES OF 36 TO 40 TOOTH COLUMNS, WITH 3 TO 5 TEETH STACKED IN EACH ONE

NEEDED TO EAT
400KG
OF VEGGIES
EVERY DAY

DEFENCE RATING
7

BRACHIOSAURUS

Just like giraffes, the Brachiosaurus was able to reach high into treetop canopies to find its lunch. Which was lucky, because it needed to eat 400kg of plant matter every day. The height of two double-decker buses, these jumbo-sized Jurassic grazers had spoon-shaped teeth perfect for scooping and scraping the tops of trees bare – this was called 'high browsing'. Tasty!

Called 'arm lizard' by scientists because its front 'arms' were longer than its hind legs, palaeontologists still have lots to learn about this ancient dino's behaviour. Was it slow and clumsy or nimble and sure-footed? They think it was warm-blooded, but how did it stay cool? Look out for updates as more is discovered.

DATA

NAME *Brakhiōn* (arm) + *sauros* (lizard)

LIVED 154–153 million years ago – late Jurassic period

SIZE 26 metres – that's longer than a cricket pitch

WEIGHT 40 tons – the same as about 20 cars

BEST DEFENCE The Brachiosaurus was big enough to swat off attacks, plus it travelled in herds

AS HEAVY AS
20 CARS

FACT EARLY EXPERTS WRONGLY GUESSED BRACHIOSAURUS LIVED IN WATER, USING ITS RAISED NOSTRILS LIKE A SNORKEL.

ANKYLOSAURUS

You wouldn't want to mess with an armoured Ankylosaurus. This hard-shelled herbivore had spiny plates called osteoderms – just like a crocodile's, they're bones that fuse together with the skin. A big brute with tiny teeth, the Ankylosaurus was one of the last dinosaurs to ever walk the Earth.

Its tail club was used to smash trees and potential threats, but even without those defences, this living tank would have been hard to take down. Unlike its tall-necked cousins, it stuck to low-lying foliage and had a fantastic nose – great for keeping a low profile and sniffing out trouble.

DATA

NAME *Ankylos* (curved) + *sauros* (lizard)

LIVED 83-66 million years ago – the very late Cretaceous period

SIZE 8 metres – two times the length of a car

WEIGHT 4 tons – that's as heavy as two giraffes

BEST DEFENCE Its tough outer shell. Just look at it!

FACT ONE FOSSIL LOOKED SO MUCH LIKE A MONSTER FROM THE GHOSTBUSTERS MOVIES, SCIENTISTS NAMED IT AFTER IT – ZUUL CRURIVASTATOR. SPOOKY!

DEFENCE RATING
10

HEAVY AS 2 GIRAFFES

OSTEODERMS

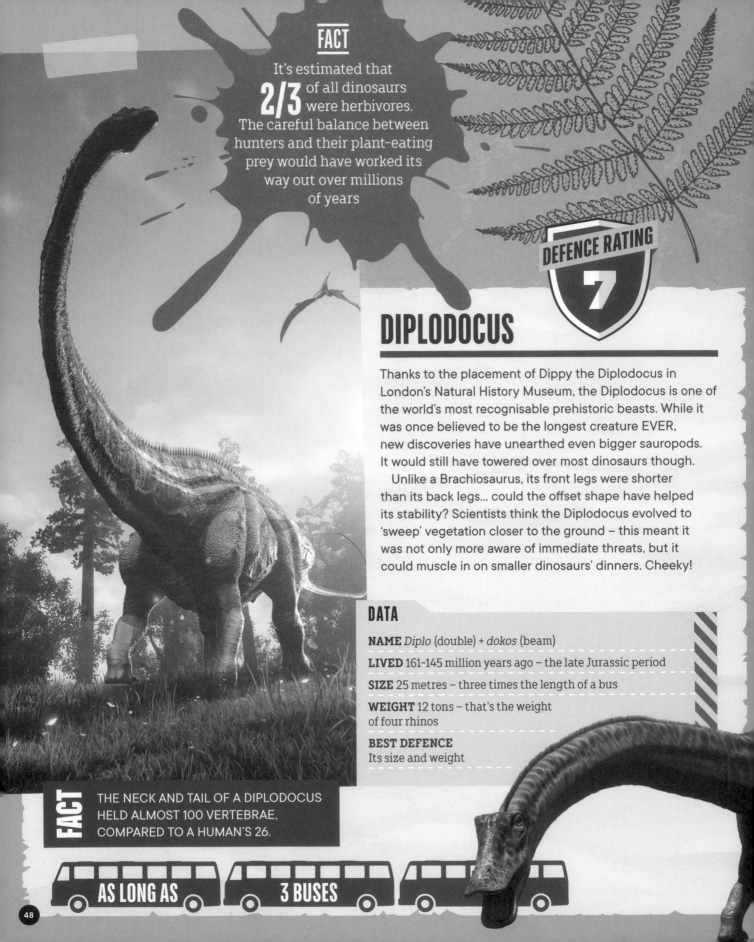

FACT

It's estimated that **2/3** of all dinosaurs were herbivores. The careful balance between hunters and their plant-eating prey would have worked its way out over millions of years

DEFENCE RATING

7

DIPLODOCUS

Thanks to the placement of Dippy the Diplodocus in London's Natural History Museum, the Diplodocus is one of the world's most recognisable prehistoric beasts. While it was once believed to be the longest creature EVER, new discoveries have unearthed even bigger sauropods. It would still have towered over most dinosaurs though.

Unlike a Brachiosaurus, its front legs were shorter than its back legs... could the offset shape have helped its stability? Scientists think the Diplodocus evolved to 'sweep' vegetation closer to the ground – this meant it was not only more aware of immediate threats, but it could muscle in on smaller dinosaurs' dinners. Cheeky!

DATA

NAME *Diplo* (double) + *dokos* (beam)

LIVED 161-145 million years ago – the late Jurassic period

SIZE 25 metres – three times the length of a bus

WEIGHT 12 tons – that's the weight of four rhinos

BEST DEFENCE
Its size and weight

FACT

THE NECK AND TAIL OF A DIPLODOCUS HELD ALMOST 100 VERTEBRAE, COMPARED TO A HUMAN'S 26.

AS LONG AS   **3 BUSES**

HADROSAURUS

The Hadrosaurus is often called the 'duck-billed' dinosaur thanks to its curious muzzle. It explored what is now east America using its shovel-shaped nose to dig at lush vegetation to gnaw on, and scientists used to think it rested on its tail like a kangaroo!

Over the years, the Hadrosaurus has caused lots of scientific head scratching, mainly because they've only found one skeleton. It was the first mostly complete dinosaur fossil found in North America and is a good example of how we used to look to modern-day animals to help identify species from the past. Its soft body would have made it an easy treat for most carnivores – it relied on its fast feet to get away.

DATA

NAME *Hadros* (bulky) + *sauros* (lizard)

LIVED 80-75 million years ago – the end of the Cretaceous period

SIZE 9 metres long – the length of a telephone pole

WEIGHT 7 tons – the same as a rhinoceros

BEST DEFENCE Super sprinter

FACT THE HADROSAURUS IS FAMOUS FOR BEING THE FIRST EVER DINO SKELETON TO BE DISPLAYED IN 3D IN 1868, NOT LAID OUT FLAT.

DUCK-LIKE MUZZLE

DEFENCE RATING
5

FEARSOME FLYERS

They might not have been dinos, but these ancient reptiles certainly soared! Long before birds filled the air above us, pterosaurs ruled the skies. United by their feathers, advanced forearms and hollow bones, they really were winged wonders

ZHEJIANGOPTERUS

DANGER 6 RATING

With its big, boneless beak, the Zhejiangopterus looked like a scary, modern-day shoebill. Similar to some other of these fearsome flyers, it shuffled around using its wings to explore rockpools and wet areas in what is now China, a bit like a stork.

A medium-sized pterosaur, unlike many of its Cretaceous cousins it had no crest and due to the size of its bulbous head, some scientists think it would have been a particularly unstable flyer. It needed extra-strong muscles to balance the weight of its head against the rest of its body.

DATA

NAME *Zhejiang* (a coastal province in modern day China) + *pteron* (wing)

LIVED 83-70 million years ago – late Cretaceous period

SIZE 5 metre wingspan – like two Christmas trees on top of one another

WEIGHT 8kg – that's the weight of a microwave

FIERCE THREAT The Zhejiangopterus walked like a stork – it would have been fast in a fight

FACT THE ZHEJIANGOPTERUS HAD LOTS OF HOLLOW SPACE IN ITS BEAK TO KEEP IT LIGHTWEIGHT

QUETZALCOATLUS

The Quetzalcoatlus was named after a feathered Aztec god and it's easy to see why. One of the largest flying animals of all time, this immense reptile had an unusually long neck and no teeth, meaning its beak was extra sharp. The size of a small plane, it scoured the skies all over the world in the Mesozoic age.

Its wings were so tough, scientists think it may have bent them to walk on all fours, stalking its prey on land or in small streams. Look out for future discoveries about the Quetzalcoatlus: just a few full skeletons have been discovered and it's likely scientists will find out more about this flyer as new fossils are found.

DATA

NAME Named after Quetzalcoatl – an Aztec serpent god

LIVED 68 million years ago – late Cretaceous period

SIZE 12 metre wingspan – that's the same size as a Brachiosaurus

WEIGHT Up to 250kg – seven times the weight of the great bustard, the heaviest flying bird

FIERCE THREAT Its sharp and pointed beak! Using its long neck, it homed in on unsuspecting prey

FACT ITS BEAK WAS LONGER THAN THE HEIGHT OF A HUMAN. IT COULD DO SOME SERIOUS DAMAGE!

PTERODACTYLUS

Can you picture your little fingers stretching out to form leathery wings like a bat… but much bigger? The Pterodactylus is named 'winged finger', and that's why. One of the most famous flyers of all time, it was the first ever pterosaur discovered, way back in 1784.

As our understanding of the natural world has evolved, the way we view these ancient animals has also changed – scientists once thought the Pterodactylus was a sea beast that used its wings as flippers! Today studies have suggested it's more likely to have roamed the land on all fours, a bit like a vampire bat, using its strong flight muscles to launch itself into the air.

NAME *Pteron* (winged) + *daktulos* (finger)

LIVED 150–144 million years ago – late Jurassic period

SIZE 1 metre wingspan – only about the length of a guitar

WEIGHT 5kg – like an Italian Greyhound with wings…!

FIERCE THREAT Its 90 short, sharp teeth could grind up fish and smaller dinosaurs

FACT THANKS TO THE MOVIES, YOU MIGHT KNOW THESE BEASTS AS PTERODACTYLS – BUT THAT'S THEIR WIDER FAMILY NAME.

DANGER
5
RATING

DANGER
8
RATING

HEAVY AS A
BISON

PTERANODON

Much bigger than its older family friend the Pterodactylus, the Pteranodon was a toothless dragon that most likely ate fish – and a lot of them! Why were so many pterosaurs piscivores (fish-eaters)? Species evolve to best suit their environment – and where dinosaurs had the land covered in the late Cretaceous period, open waters would have been full of fish for these flying predators to feed on.

Unlike some species, so many Pteranodons have been found that scientists have a pretty good idea of their overall appearance. As tall as a human, these furry, fearsome flyers flew in huge flocks and scouted fish from up high over the ocean. Can you imagine seeing a flock of them in the wild today?

DATA

NAME *Pteron* (winged) + *an* (without) + *odont* (teeth)

LIVED 85-75 million years ago – late Cretaceous period

SIZE 10 metre wingspan – that's two saltwater crocodiles stacked end to end

WEIGHT 25kg – the same as a baby American bison

FIERCE THREAT Their razor-sharp beaks! The Pteranodon would spear fish underwater

ZZZZZ...

FACT THERE'S A THEORY THAT PTERANODONS MIGHT HAVE BEEN ABLE TO SLEEP WHILE AIRBORNE

DANGER
9
RATING

RHAMPHORHYNCHUS

One of the weirdest looking winged reptiles, the Rhamphorhynchus was discovered in 1846 and named after the curved snout shape of its beak. Unlike other pterosaurs, it had a rudder on its tail that allowed it to 'steer' in the air. Tailless pterosaurs had a LOT less control over their flying and probably looked pretty awkward taking off.

Some Rhamphorhynchus fossils are so well preserved that palaeontologists know loads about them. Even its internal organs have been accounted for – crazy for something 150 million years old! In comparison, the oldest human skeletons are only hundreds of thousands of years in age.

DATA

NAME *Rhamphos* (curved) + *rhyngchos* (beak)

LIVED 163–150 million years ago – late Jurassic period

SIZE Its wingspan was 2 metres – as long as a fridge

WEIGHT 1kg – the same as a bag of sugar

FIERCE THREAT Rhamphorhynchus's steady flight would have kept it in hot pursuit

FACT THANKS TO COMPLETE FOSSILS, SCIENTISTS EVEN KNOW ITS FAVOURITE FISH: THE EXTINCT ASPIDORHYNCHUS. AS YOU CAN SEE, IT WAS VERY LONG!

HATZEGOPTERYX

Imagine a fish-chomping giraffe flying towards you at super speed! This enormous pterosaur – one of the largest ever to have lived – was found in Transylvania in 2012. It would have soared over prehistoric Europe, although scientists think it was so big it may have needed a run-up to get off the ground.

The Hatzegopteryx had double the wingspan of an albatross, meaning its hunting ground had a massive range. Its fossils were found on the far-out Hatzeg Island, which had scientists scratching their heads – the island's dinosaurs were dwarf-sized, so how come the Hatzegopteryx was so big? What do you think?

DATA

NAME *Hatzeg* (a region in modern-day Romania) + *pteryx* (wing)

LIVED 70-66 million years ago – late Cretaceous period

SIZE 10 metre wingspan – the height of a telephone pole

WEIGHT 250kg – the same as a medium-sized pig

FIERCE THREAT The Hatzegopteryx's mammoth size made it a HUGE danger for its smaller prey

FACT WHAT DID HATZEGOPTERYX EAT? EXPERTS CAN'T DECIDE IF IT WAS FISH OR THE TINY DINOS ON HATZEG ISLAND

DANGER 8 RATING

While mighty dinosaurs dominated the land, enormous reptiles patrolled the oceans. There were three main groups – plesiosaurs, ichthyosaurs and mosasaurs – and all of them were fearsome predators

SEA MONSTERS

THE LENGTH OF FIVE COWS

PLESIOSAURS

Although they ranged in size from two to fifteen metres in length (that's about the same as three cars end to end) plesiosaurs weren't dinos – most had round bodies with four flippers, a tail and wickedly sharp teeth. Breathing air and feeding mostly on huge fish and other marine reptiles, these incredible swimmers ruled the prehistoric seas for around 150 million years.

DATA

NAME Elasmosaurus; *Elasmos* (to attack) + *saurus* (reptile)

LIVED 85-66 million years ago – late Cretaceous period

SIZE 13 metres – the length of five cows

WEIGHT More than 2,000kg – that's 20 baby elephants

FIERCE THREAT Elasmosaurus used its long, bendy neck to get close to prey without them noticing

FACT MORE THAN HALF OF ITS LENGTH WAS ITS NECK. IT WAS SO LONG THAT WHEN SCIENTISTS FIRST STUDIED AN ELASMOSAURUS SKELETON THEY THOUGHT THE NECK WAS ITS TAIL. THEY PUT ITS HEAD ON THE WRONG END. WHOOPS!

ICHTHYOSAURS

These dolphin-shaped reptiles flourished in the Mesozoic era's warm, shallow seas, usually growing to four or five metres in length. With a long jaw and a mouth full of sharp teeth, they used their streamlined bodies, flat flippers and powerful tails to speed after large fish and squid. Just try not to get speared!

BIG AS A BLUE WHALE

DATA

NAME Shonisaurus – after Shoshone Mountain in Nevada, US, where it was discovered in 1920

LIVED 216-203 million years ago – late Triassic period

SIZE A whopping 21 metres – that's almost as big as a blue whale today. Who would win in a swim-off?

WEIGHT 80,000kg – as heavy as two sperm whales

FIERCE THREAT Its size! The Shonisaurus was GIANT

FACT THE FIRST COMPLETE ICHTHYOSAURUS WAS FOUND BY A 12-YEAR-OLD! TURN TO P84 TO FIND OUT MORE ABOUT HER...

MOSASAURS

LONG AS AN HGV

These gigantic marine lizards, similar to flippered crocodiles, were the supreme killers of the Cretaceous period, often reaching the size of whales. Sneaky and slow-moving, they crept up on ammonites, turtles and even other mosasaurs in shallow waters, snaring prey in heavy, deadly jaws loaded with curved, knife-like teeth.

DATA

NAME Mosasaurus – named after the Meuse river that flows through France, Belgium and the Netherlands

LIVED 70-66 million years ago, during the late Cretaceous period

SIZE 10 metres – almost as long as an HGV trailer

WEIGHT 14,000kg – that's the same as four hippos

FIERCE THREAT It had teeth at the back of its mouth that pointed inwards to keep prey from escaping

FACT MOSASAURS WERE TOP PREHISTORIC PREDATORS, BUT THEY COULD STILL BE ATTACKED – ONE MOSASAUR FOSSIL SHOWS A SHARK BITE MARK IN ITS SPINE. SAVAGE!

TERROR BIRDS

Not all ancient birds flew. Today, we know the phorusrhacids as the terror birds – it's easy to see why! Although these carnivorous hunters varied in size, they were ALWAYS vicious and became real apex predators in what is now North America. In fact, between its 25 species, the phorusrhaciade family survived for 60 million years

AT CLOSE RANGE

Phorusrhacids existed after many of the species you'll see in this issue, in an age called the Cenozoic era. It leads right up into modern times, containing lots of ancient creatures that evolved into the animals we know today.

TERROR ON TWO FEET

These beaked predators were built for fighting. While avian evolution might not have given them jaws as powerful as carnivore theropods, terror birds could hold their own thanks to blade-like beaks. Fast runners make for amazing hunters, and scientists think they outran smaller prey and brought them down by pecking, kicking and using their beaks to stab.

FAST AND FLIGHTLESS

Terror birds were stocky brutes that shared many characteristics with dodos and today's flightless birds. Their hardy frames focused on their most lethal parts: long necks and legs. Research shows that their powerful stance would have been great for hunting, with some sprinting up to 48km/h – the same as an emu today. Just imagine an emu with a knife for a nose!

DID YOU *know?*

Instead of chewing, the phorusrhacids would swallow their prey whole if possible... and then throw up the indigestible remains, just like an owl. Yuck!

▲ Gastornis fossil

59

KILLER CROCS

RULING REPTILES

For more than 150 million years, the planet was dominated by a group of animals called archosaurs (also known as the ruling reptiles). The dinosaurs are the best-known members of this group, but crocodiles belong to it too. Fossils show that the ancient ancestors of modern crocodiles first walked the Earth 200 million years ago.

Turns out these powerful predators haven't changed much in 200 million years! Here's how the snappy species evolved...

◀ Archosaur

TOOTHY TIMELINE

252-201 MILLION YEARS AGO
TRIASSIC

Archosaurs thrived in this period and some (especially a group called phytosaurs) looked similar to crocodiles, with long jaws, many teeth and scaly, armoured skin. The earliest croc ancestors, a group called the protosuchians, evolved at the end of this period. They were very different to the crocodiles we're familiar with today. Most were less than a metre long and they lived on land.

201-145 MILLION YEARS AGO
JURASSIC

Several species that could be considered early crocodiles lived in this period. There were many more species of croc than there are today and they varied widely in their appearance and habits. Some ate insects, some were land-based carnivores and others were plant-eaters. A few had also moved into the oceans, like the Dakosaurus.

145-66 MILLION YEARS AGO
CRETACEOUS

The family tree split: on one branch was the Deinosuchus, on another was the enormous Sarcosuchus and on a third branch were the Eusuchians, or 'true crocodiles'. During this phase they started moving into the water – their bodies stretched out and they developed the flat, toothy snouts and powerful jaws we know so well today.

▲ Dakosaurus

1 EXTINCT ANCESTOR

NAME Deinosuchus (which means 'terrible crocodile' in Greek)

STATUS An extinct ancestor of the crocodile and alligator that died out 82 million years ago

DIET Sea turtles and dinosaurs

CLAIM TO FAME Hunting live tyrannosaurs! Fossilised bones of two tyrannosaurs found in North America show bite marks that match the giant teeth of the Deinosuchus. One of the wounds had started to heal, proving these crocs were picking fights with live dinosaurs... and living to fight another day.

2 COLOSSAL COUSIN

NAME Sarcosuchus – 'the flesh crocodile'

STATUS A distant crocodilian cousin that died out 112 million years ago

DIET Prehistoric fish

CLAIM TO FAME It never stopped growing. Today's crocodiles max out when they reach adulthood (aged around 10), but the Sarcosuchus just kept getting bigger and bigger. Palaeontologists studying growth rings in its bones have found that this gigantic reptile grew steadily throughout its lifetime. The largest reached lengths of over 12 metres and weighed a whopping 10 tons. That's one colossal croc!

3 MODERN MARVEL

NAME Saltwater or estuarine crocodile

STATUS Thriving in saltwater and freshwater regions of eastern India, Southeast Asia and northern Australia

DIET Crabs, fish, birds, turtles, pigs and buffalo... They have even been known to eat the odd human!

CLAIM TO FAME The biggest living reptile in the world, adult males can grow to 7 metres in length – that's three times as long as a full-sized bed. They also have the strongest bite of any animal on the planet. Don't get in the way of these jaws...

THE SARCOSUCHUS HAD A BITE FORCE OF

88,000 NEWTONS

COMPARED TO A HUMAN'S WIMPY 1,300

MEET
THE MEG

Possibly the biggest (and most terrifying) fish to have ever evolved, the Megalodon – AKA Megatooth – was so large that it ate whales for tea

DINNER

UH-OH!

DATA

NAME Megalodon

LIVED 20-3 million years ago – the Cenozoic era

SIZE 15-18 metres – the length of a cricket pitch

WEIGHT 50,000kg – that's 625 fully grown people

FIERCE THREAT Absolutely its bone-splintering bite!

LENGTH OF A CRICKET PITCH

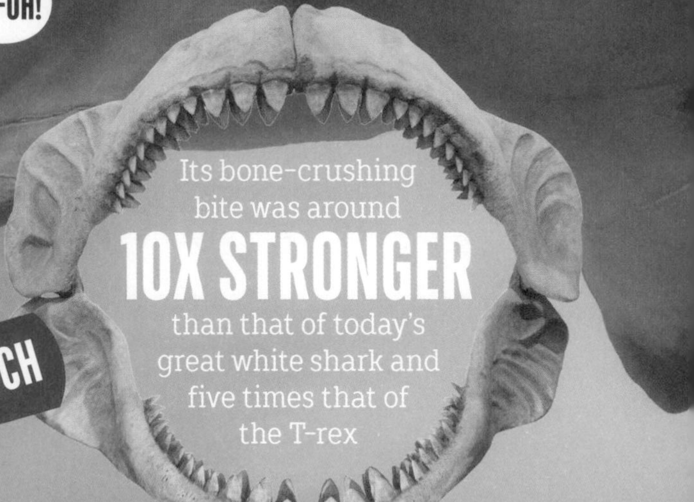

Its bone-crushing bite was around **10X STRONGER** than that of today's great white shark and five times that of the T-rex

THE SIZE OF DINNER PLATES

276 TEETH

18 CMS LONG

A STORY OF SHARKS

Sharks have a long evolutionary history, appearing in the seas before trees even existed

ACANTHODIANS
(410 MILLION YEARS AGO)

CLADOSELACHE
(380 MILLION YEARS AGO)

STETHACANTHUS
(359 MILLION YEARS AGO)

HEXANCHIFORMES
(195 MILLION YEARS AGO)

MAKO
(45 MILLION YEARS AGO)

HAMMERHEAD
(20 MILLION YEARS AGO)

RENEWABLE RAZORS

Megalodon isn't called the Megatooth shark for nothing – its monstrous jaws were lined with 276 needle-sharp teeth, reaching up to 18cm in length. These spiky gnashers were shed continuously and replaced by new ones – the Meg could get through as many as 40,000 in its lifetime. Unsurprisingly, almost all Megalodon fossil remains are teeth.

GREAT WHITE

MEGALODON

63

FROZEN
FORESTS

It's not just the bones of dinosaurs or other ancient creatures that have been preserved for millions of years under soil, sea and rock. Entire forests have been fossilised, too

During the late Triassic period, 225 million years ago, the 'Dawn of the Dinosaurs' saw early dinos and reptiles roaming the Earth, and prehistoric forests with giant, soaring trees reaching to the skies.

Petrified Forest National Park in Arizona, US, is one of the world's best places to see remnants of the ancient trees that once covered large regions of Earth's surface. During the Triassic period, Arizona was home to lush, tropical rainforests, bursting with plants called ferns, horsetails and cycads, and towering conifer trees.

As the land and climate changed over millions of years, sculpted by water and wind, these forests gave way to the barren, rocky desert you'll find here today. But look closely while wandering through this national park, and you'll discover that many of the glistening rocks are actually tree trunks, branches and leaves.

These Triassic fossilised – or 'petrified' – trees have been buried under layers of sediment from lakes and rivers, absorbing water and silica (a natural substance found in rocks, clay, sand and volcanic ash), which crystallised over time into a hard, glittering mineral known as quartz. Around 40 different minerals have been found in the petrified wood discovered around the world, including silica, calcite and pyrite.

FOSSIL FOREST

The oldest known fossil forest dates back to the Devonian period 385 million years ago – it was discovered in the Catskill Mountains in New York, US, in the 1920s. Fossils of hundreds of large tree stumps were uncovered in a quarry as workers extracted rock to build the nearby Gilboa Dam. The incredible Gilboa Forest revealed fossils of some of Earth's oldest trees, along with animals that lived in the ancient sea bordering the forest. Wood you believe it?

EXPLOSIVE FIND

In the Petrified Forest of Calistoga in California, US, you can see petrified redwood trees from the Pliocene epoch, which are a whopping 3.4 million years old. When nearby volcano Mount St Helena erupted, the powerful blast knocked down the giant redwoods, burying them in silica-rich volcanic ash. Water filtered through the ash, saturating the trees with silica, which perfectly preserved the wood and created a three-dimensional fossil in a process known as 'permineralisation'.

PETRIFIED FORESTS EXIST ACROSS THE WORLD AND ANCIENT TREES, NOW TURNED TO STONE, CAN BE FOUND ON EVERY CONTINENT

ANCIENT WOODLANDS

In Wales, the petrified remains of an ancient forest can be seen stretching across the beach at Borth, where the stumps of pine, alder, oak and birch trees rise up from the sand. Believed to be up to 5,000 years old, this submerged woodland remained preserved in peat (decayed vegetation) until a MASSIVE storm blew away tons of sand and revealed the ancient wonder in 2014.

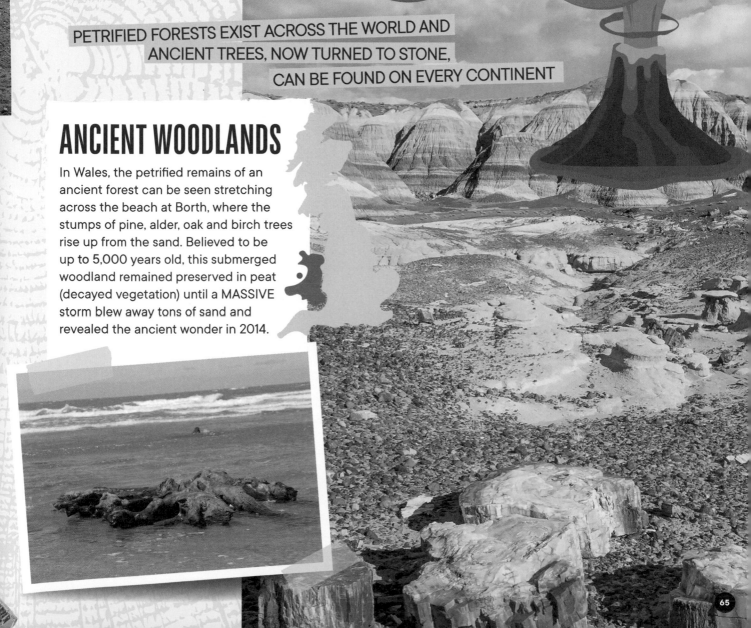

HORSETAILS

Related to ferns, when you see horsetails in spring, the stems look a little like asparagus. Then in the summer, feathery upright shoots appear which, as the name suggests, look a lot like a horse's tail. The rough stems of these ancient plants have horizontal bands similar to bamboo. Long before scouring pads were on supermarket shelves, people tied bunches of horsetails together and used them to clean pots and pans. How's that for eco-friendly?

Prehistoric Plant Life

Follow our nature trail and see how many plants you recognise. They all existed when dinosaurs roamed the Earth and still grow in gardens, parks and wild habitats today. Why not track one of them down? They outlasted the dinosaurs and they're still thriving now

GINKGO TREES

Ginkgo trees have unique, fan-shaped leaves that turn a bright yellow colour in the autumn and fruit that smells similar to... rancid butter?! Thought to have existed for 245 million years, it's one of the world's oldest living tree species. Ginkgo leaves are used in Chinese herbal medicine to help improve people's memory. They can grow to a height of 24 metres – that's almost twice as tall as a Brachiosaurus.

FERNS

Ferns have been around for 350 million years, so these prehistoric plants are actually older than dinosaurs. In fact, once upon a time, ferns were the primary vegetation covering the Earth. Some varieties grew in vast swamps and sank to the bottom when they died – the coal we use today was formed from this dead plant material. One hardy woodland fern is the hart's-tongue fern that has glossy green leaves with orange spores on their undersides, and little marks reminiscent of a centipede's legs.

MONKEY PUZZLE TREES

A word of warning if you see this quirky tree: according to legend, anyone who speaks when passing a monkey puzzle will either get bad luck or grow a monkey's tail. Its green leaves are stiff and spiky, but the Jurassic dinosaurs didn't seem to mind and happily munched away. The tree was given its current common name in the 19th century when a British barrister saw it for the first time and commented that even a monkey would be bamboozled when climbing the spiralling branches.

MAGNOLIAS

Shut your eyes and smell a magnolia flower. Do you think you're standing in a sweet shop next to the sherbet lemons or Parma violets? Loved for their sweet floral fragrance, magnolias were one of the first flowering plants, evolving towards the end of the dinosaur age. In those days, however, the flowers weren't pollinated by bees as these garden insects didn't exist yet. The important job of transferring pollen was a task for beetles.

**LIKE PEPPER WITH YOUR FOOD?
THE FIRST BLACK PEPPER PLANTS GREW
145 MILLION YEARS AGO**

PROTEAS

The national flower of South Africa and native to the country, proteas are thought to be one of the oldest families of flowering plants on the planet, dating back 300 million years. It's estimated there are over 1,300 species. Common king varieties are usually a pink-red colour and are the same shape as a type of artichoke. Proteas are named after Proteus, the son of the Greek god Poseidon.

CYCADS

Today's many different cycad species are thought to have evolved from a prehistoric plant that is now totally extinct. Some look like palm trees, others are similar to ferns, but they all typically have short trunks topped off with a green crown of large leaves. Certain types of cycads are known as bread trees because they contain a starchy substance that can be extracted and eaten as a food. There are also varieties that produce dangerous toxins, so beware.

DID YOU *know?*

Herbivorous dinosaurs needed to eat around 400kg of this stuff every day just to keep moving – that's compared to the 1.8kg humans eat on average each day.

MEGA BEASTS

Make way for the mega beasts. Huge prehistoric mammals that filled the footprints of the dinosaurs, these super-sized animals may look like today's predators... but they're so much mightier. One thing's for sure: they would NOT have made great pets!

GIANT GROUND SLOTH

Think of sloths today and you'll probably picture tired, tree-hugging forest bears – this wasn't always the case. The Giant Ground Sloth looked more like a long-nosed grizzly bear than today's smaller sloths. Bigger than an elephant, it was one of history's largest land mammals.

The Giant Ground Sloth would have shuffled on its great claws and ground down leaves, twigs and nuts with its large, blunt teeth – they never stopped growing! You might not expect it, but this massive mammal was probably a picky eater... scientists have guessed this because of its narrow lips. It used them like a pair of pincers to avoid poisonous plants.

DATA

NAME Megatherium; *Mega* (great) + *thorium* (beast)

LIVED 65,000-12,000 years ago – the middle to late Pleistocene epoch

SIZE 6 metres – that's six times longer than the biggest modern sloth

WEIGHT Up to 4 tons – about the same weight as a hippopotamus

SURVIVAL SKILL
Some species of giant sloths had osteoderms under their skin – bony deposits, like natural chain mail

HEAVY AS A HIPPO

FACT GIANT GROUND SLOTH MEGALONYX JEFFERSONII WAS NAMED AFTER THIRD AMERICAN PRESIDENT THOMAS JEFFERSON IN 1822

6X SMALLER!

TOP SPEED
70KM/H

LONG AS A
CAR

GIANT SHORT-FACED BEAR

This short-snouted savage would have dwarfed today's bears. In fact, scientists believe it might have been the largest flesh-eating mammal ever to have lived in America. Mammoth bones indented with the Giant Short-faced Bear's teeth marks have been found in Colorado, proving any meat was on the menu for this hairy hulk.

It's also thought the bear used its raw strength to hurl itself at its enemies. Given that it could run at 70km/h, you wouldn't want to be there when it caught up with you. Nobody's sure why it became extinct, but we do know that it crossed over in history with humans. As larger prey died out, it probably couldn't find enough food to survive.

DATA

NAME Arctodus simus; *Arctos* (bear) + *odus* (tooth) + *simus* (blunt-nosed)

LIVED 1.8 million–11,000 years ago – the middle Pleistocene epoch

SIZE 4 metres – about the same length as a car

WEIGHT 1 ton – the same as a polar bear

SURVIVAL SKILL Its colossal size and explosive sprint would have made it a truly terrifying opponent

FACT THEIR SHORT SNOUTS AREN'T SO SHORT. IT'S AN ILLUSION CAUSED BY THEIR DEEP FACE

**THE WEIGHT OF
2X LIMOUSINES**

BP means
BEFORE PRESENT
It's the time scale scientists use to point to an age before our own without homing in on an exact year

MASTODON

An ancestor of the elephant, the hairy Mastodon may look like a woolly mammoth, but it's a separate species entirely. Like so many prehistoric beasts in this issue, they lived in wildly different time periods – the woolly mammoth lived between 5 million and 4,000 years ago. The Mastodon marched across the whole world 20 million years or so earlier, but their similar traits prove just how well both beasts handled our prehistoric planet. Mastodons were mighty!

With a mouth full of big, cone-shaped molars, the Mastodon may have looked ready to take down any enemy, but it had a completely herbivorous diet. With no meat on the menu, it used its 2.5 metre tusks for fending off predators and fighting for the perfect Mastodon mate. Starting out in America, they eventually spread across the world – its hairy hide worked like a big woolly jumper to help it survive, even in the coldest climates.

DATA

NAME Mastodon; *Mastós* (breast) + *odon* (tooth)

LIVED 23 million–11,700 years ago – early Miocene to the Pleistocene epoch

SIZE 3 metres – taller than a full-size Christmas tree

WEIGHT 6 tons – the same weight as two limousines

SURVIVAL SKILL Their tusks weren't just for show. Predators could see how hard they were to hunt

FACT WHEN MASTODON BONES WERE FOUND IN 1705, SOME PEOPLE THOUGHT THEY BELONGED TO HUMAN GIANTS.

ANDREWSARCHUS

Is it a lion... or a massive vole? Well, it's neither. Since its skull was discovered in 1923, scientists have argued about many aspects of the Andrewsarchus – what we *can* be sure of is that its teeth were terrifyingly strong. This stocky fighter looked like a long-nosed hyena, but it had hoofed toes. Hooves still help animals travel great distances and protect their feet, so it's likely it searched high and low for prey to terrorise.

Since it was discovered along the shoreline, it could have scoured rock pools and used its powerful jaws to crack into turtle shells and snails. So why was it called Andrew? It's named after the explorer Roy Chapman Andrew, who led an exploration to Mongolia. Hopefully, he wasn't as scary!

DATA

30X HEAVIER

NAME Andrewsarchus mongoliensis; (Roy Chapman) *Andrew + archos* (leader)

LIVED 45-36 million years ago – the Eocene epoch

SIZE 2 metres – as tall as a grown man

WEIGHT 900kg – 30 times heavier than a Dalmatian

SURVIVAL SKILL Those massive, bone-cracking teeth. Compared to its body, they were super-sized

FACT THE ANDREWSARCHUS' CLOSEST LIVING RELATIVES COULD BE GOATS AND SHEEP. IT'S A WOLF IN SHEEP'S CLOTHING

AS TALL AS A MAN

SURVIVORS!

These incredible creatures have stood the test of time – their appearance has hardly changed in millions of years! Looking at these guys gives us a glimpse of what ancient worlds were like long ago...

HORSESHOE CRAB

They don't get much more prehistoric than the horseshoe crab. One of evolution's supreme survivors, it's been scuttling across our ocean floors for 450 million years. They look like crabs but are actually part of the arachnid family, so more closely related to spiders, scorpions and ticks. Today the medical world uses their blue blood to test for dangerous bacteria in drugs and vaccines. If you've ever had a vaccine, you can thank the horseshoe crab for keeping you safe.

450 million years old

X10

FACT HORSESHOE CRABS HAVE EYES EVERYWHERE – 10 ALTOGETHER.

PURPLE FROG

120 million years old

Only officially named by scientists in 2003, the purple frog is thought to have existed for 120 million years, dating back to the break up of the supercontinent Gondwana. Today it's incredibly difficult to find as it spends most of its life underground, appearing for just a few days at the start of India's monsoon season.

FACT PURPLE FROGS ARE UNDER THREAT FROM DEFORESTATION AND LOCAL COMMUNITIES WHO EAT THE TADPOLES AND MAKE AMULETS TO CALM THEIR CHILDREN WHEN STORMS COME. SADLY FOR PURPLE FROGS, THEY'RE NOT POISONOUS.

CASSOWARY

If you want to know what a dinosaur foot looked like, take a glimpse at the cassowary's colossal scaly tootsies! This incredible species is a direct dinosaur descendant and the three huge, dagger-like claws on each foot make it as deadly as any Velociraptor. Found in the tropical forests of Southeast Asia and Australia, the flightless bird grows up to two metres tall. It can deliver a powerful kick if it feels threatened, and running away won't help: these birds can sprint at over 50km an hour.

60 million years old

50KM/H

FACT BIRDS ARE DESCENDANTS OF THE ONLY DINOSAURS TO SURVIVE THE CRETACEOUS MASS EXTINCTION, WHICH TOOK PLACE 66 MILLION YEARS AGO

95% WATER

JELLYFISH

500 million years old

Jellyfish don't have brains, hearts or eyes, and they've remained more or less the same for 500 million years – maybe even longer! Almost completely made of water (95%), they're CLEARLY doing something right as they've survived all of Earth's mass extinction events and actually look set to increase in population as climate change takes hold and their predators disappear.

FACT BECAUSE JELLYFISH TEND TO JUST FOLLOW CURRENTS, THEY CAN THRIVE IN EVERY CORNER OF THE PLANET – FROM WARM TROPICAL WATERS TO THE COLD ARCTIC DEPTHS. THEY'RE ADAPTABLE.

PIG-NOSED TURTLE

140 million years old

With an unusual snout that makes it look like an alien, the pig-nosed turtle is one of a kind. It uses its special nostrils as a snorkel at the surface and unlike other freshwater turtles has flippers instead of legs, making it specially adapted to life in the water. Although it's been with us for around 140 million years, it's so cute that it's now in danger from the exotic pet trade.

FACT MALE PIG-NOSED TURTLES SPEND THEIR WHOLE LIVES IN THE WATER AND FEMALES ONLY LEAVE TO NEST

LARGEST LIZARDS ON EARTH

4 million years old

KOMODO DRAGON

Don't believe in dragons? They're real! Giant, ancient reptiles rule on the remote island of Komodo and a few neighbouring isles in Indonesia. Growing up to three metres long, komodo dragons are the largest lizards on Earth, with scaly skin, super-long forked tongues, large sharp teeth and a deadly bite that infects their victim with venomous proteins, killing it within days. It may not fly or breathe fire, but this dragon is as dangerous as a Hungarian Horntail!

FACT YOU'LL FIND THEM IN KOMODO, BUT THERE'S NEW EVIDENCE THAT THE KOMODO DRAGON ALSO LIVED IN AUSTRALIA ABOUT 4 MILLION YEARS AGO

20 million years old

BABIRUSA

Waddling somewhere between a hippopotamus and a deer, the bizarre and brilliant babirusa is no ordinary boar. With a fat belly stacked atop dainty, deer-like legs, it has evolved free from any enemies on remote Indonesian islands – one of the reasons it has lasted so long. The babirusa looks positively naked, armed with looping tusks that are especially curious... the male's grisly grill can actually curl back and dig straight into its face. Ouch!

FACT EARLY ON DURING EVOLUTION, BABIRUSA PIGS BRANCHED OFF FROM THE REST OF THE FAMILY. WEIRDLY, THEY'VE GOT TWO-CHAMBERED DIGESTIVE SYSTEMS – MORE LIKE SHEEP.

LOOKS CAN BE DECEIVING...

It might seem as if these species have stopped evolving, but that isn't really the case – animals may look similar to their ancient ancestors, but their DNA shows they've evolved in lots of other ways, becoming resistant to diseases or behaving differently.

CROCODILES

200 million years old

Crocodiles today look remarkably similar to how they looked 200 million years ago, even though they have lots of lesser-known relatives that became extinct – crocodilians once sprinted on their toes, lived in the sea and even climbed trees. Some scientists think crocodiles have kept the same body shape for such a long time because it works so well for them... they only adapt when they're forced to by their environment.

FACT CROCODILES ARE THE CLOSEST LIVING RELATIVE OF BIRDS – IT'S THOUGHT A COMMON ANCESTOR EXISTED AROUND 240 MILLION YEARS AGO.

THE LAST DINOSAURS

Why did birds survive when the dinosaurs died out?

UNLIKELY ANCESTORS

It might be hard to believe when you see a sparrow hopping along a garden fence, but modern birds evolved from dinosaurs – and not the plant-eating kind! The distant relatives of the 11,000 different species of bird alive today were meat-eating theropods – that's the same group that Tyrannosaurus rex belonged to. Birds aren't descended from the T-rex itself though – around 150 million years ago, during the Jurassic period, the first birds evolved from small, feathery, raptor-like dinosaurs, becoming just another branch on the dinosaur family tree. For the next 80 million years, birds of all kinds evolved and thrived – some with teeth, and others with beaks.

DID YOU know?

Dino experts today call birds 'avian dinosaurs', and all the other types – from T-rex to Triceratops – 'non-avian'.

ARCHAEOPTERYX

HOATZIN

SURVIVAL OF A SPECIES

When the asteroid that wiped out the dinosaurs struck the Earth 66 million years ago, the collision caused a thick layer of ash and smoke to fill the air, blocking out the light. The impact also triggered a series of volcanic eruptions that made the atmosphere even murkier. Plants couldn't grow, which meant there wasn't enough food and more than 75% of species died out. Beaked birds were the only dinosaurs to survive these dark days – many other species didn't make it. Scientists think these might be the reasons why...

1 SLIGHTLY PECKISH

The birds that survived were small – no bigger than a modern mallard – which meant they needed less food. They also ate a much more varied diet than their toothy cousins, who'd mostly adapted to eat specific foods; sometimes just the leaves of a certain tree – or other dinosaurs. With food in short supply, they quickly perished. Beaked birds were able to pluck up hard foods like seeds and nuts from the destroyed forest floor. They also ate insects, fruit and fish, giving them many more ways of filling up and fuelling themselves.

2 WINGING IT

Being able to fly meant that birds could quickly escape the toxic fumes of volcanic eruptions. Flight also allowed them to travel long distances, moving from place to place to find food. Flying takes less energy than walking or running, so unlike their land-bound relations, birds could travel a long way without needing too much extra food to fuel their journey. It might not have been an easy ride for the surviving species on the planet, but its proof of just how hardy avian dinosaurs can be.

3 TOP TRANSFORMERS

Birds are incredibly adaptable. As smaller creatures, they have shorter lifespans and breed young sooner. A shorter cycle of birth, breeding and death meant they could adapt to their new environment more quickly. Within a short space of time, birds had evolved to be able to survive the challenging new conditions on Earth after the asteroid hit. Today birds live on every continent and in every environment on the planet, from the freezing Arctic to humid rainforests. See, they're adaptable.

SPOT THE DIFFERENCE
Do you see the family resemblance between these two?

ARCHAEOPTERYX

LIVED 163 million–145 million years ago - late Jurassic period

SIZE About the same as a modern chicken

DIET Likely small reptiles, mammals and insects

Thought to be one of the earliest known flying dinosaurs and the ancestor of modern birds, the Archaeopteryx was a prehistoric winged carnivore with a large tooth-filled beak, a bony tail and claws on its wings. Fossils found in limestone show its feathers were the same shape as flying birds. It probably only flew short distances though, as its muscles weren't strong enough to lift its large body for longer flights. Depending on who you ask, it's known as 'old wing', or the 'first bird'.

HOATZIN

LIVED 36 million years ago (Eocene) to the present day

SIZE Just like the Archaeopteryx – the same as a chicken

DIET Swamp plants. It digests food like a cow!

Most modern birds don't look anything like dinosaurs, but the Hoatzin of South America shares a distinctive trait with its prehistoric ancestors: Hoatzin chicks have claws on their wings. Today they live on lake edges in the Amazon jungle, making nests just above the water. They're nicknamed the stinkbird because they smell of manure. They get their pong by digesting leaves in a large crop (a storage pouch near the throat) and using smelly bacteria to break down and ferment each meal. Bad breath? More like 'bird' breath!

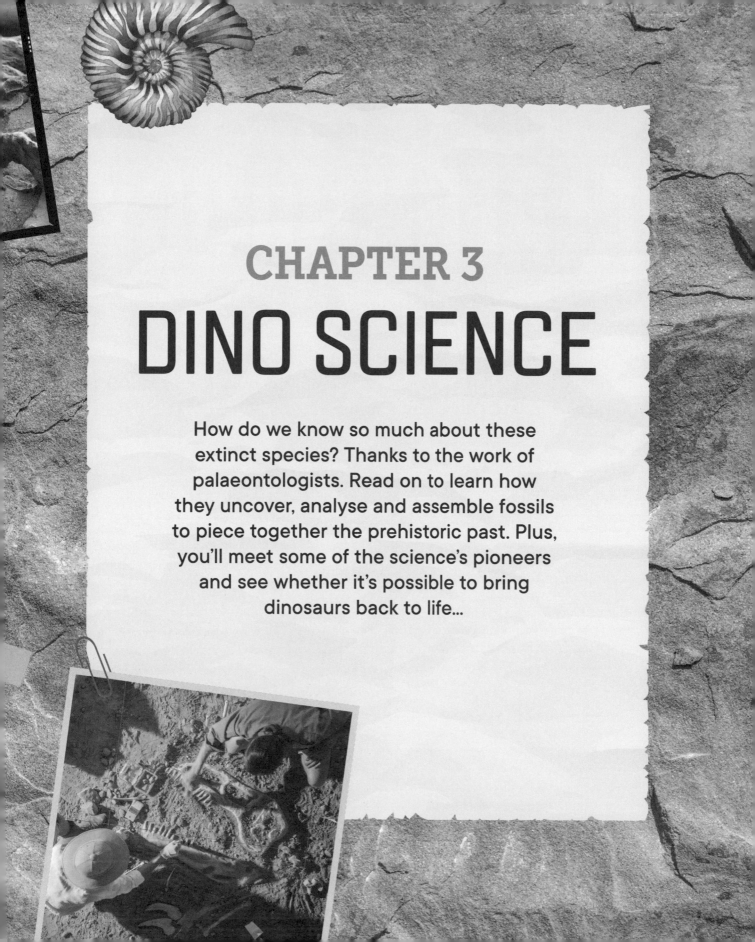

CHAPTER 3
DINO SCIENCE

How do we know so much about these extinct species? Thanks to the work of palaeontologists. Read on to learn how they uncover, analyse and assemble fossils to piece together the prehistoric past. Plus, you'll meet some of the science's pioneers and see whether it's possible to bring dinosaurs back to life...

WHAT IS PALAEONTOLOGY?

Palaeontology is the study of fossils to figure out how life has evolved on Earth. Palaeontologists use their findings alongside modern-day scientific knowledge to build a picture of ancient plants and animals – what they looked like, where they lived and even how they interacted...

PIECES OF A PUZZLE

Palaeontologists (their name means 'ancient science') don't just study dinosaur fossils, but the fossils of animals, plants and even bacteria on a quest to understand how life has evolved. The fossils they uncover often have bits missing (to count as a fossil, a discovery has to be more than 10,000 years old!), because not everything is preserved in the layers of sediment and rock when they're formed.

A key part of a palaeontologist's job, then, is to fill in these missing gaps in information. They do this by studying fossils of similar species and also those of modern-day animals for clues as to how ancient creatures might have looked and behaved. As more fossils are discovered, their understanding of prehistoric life changes and is constantly updated.

DATING GAME

Palaeontologists think the first lifeforms existed up to four billion years before humans arrived on Earth. How do they know this? Well, since the early 1900s, they've used something called 'radiometric dating' to work out how old their ancient finds are. As they age, the atoms in organic materials slowly leak energy and decay. This means scientists can tell how old something is by measuring the amount of 'energy' left in its atoms. Clever, eh?

Fossils found underground act as nature's very own time capsules, and it's not just dinosaurs they can give us clues about. The Earth's crust houses its whole history, from the most ancient rock layers that were created soon after the planet's formation to the youngest ones that are still forming today.

TITANIC TEAMWORK

Think all palaeontology is digging around in the dirt? Think again! Teams of scientists rely on scientific studies stretching back centuries. Today, some palaeontologists never even see a dig site – just like in hospitals, they use CT and X-ray scans to digitally dig into dinos, studying finds in detail and reconstructing any missing parts. Then they build 3D models of them.

Many palaeontologists still like to get their hands dirty, though. There are even dig sites you can visit – just try searching online.

DEEP DIVES

Not all fossils are found in the ground! Some specimens never left the sea, like stromatolites. They're packed with tiny microbial worlds that were once living algae. Palaeontologists believe they'll unlock key secrets to life on Earth.

HOW PALAEONTOLOGISTS FIND FOSSILS

STEP #1 Search for news of new discoveries. Builders and dog walkers are historically great at finding things in the ground.

STEP #2 Check out the dig site. Workers help them to dig fossils up in a big lump with drills, hammers and chisels. You've got to be careful they don't break.

STEP #3 Some palaeontologists specialise in delicately clearing away rock from new discoveries with special tools, which can take weeks.

STEP #4 Scientists measure, draw and photograph their new discoveries. Careful records are kept of the fossil's features.

STEP #5 All of this information is used in labs to piece the skeleton together. Then, the fossil is carefully set and placed in protective casing, ready for research. Once the work is done, some of them are then moved to museums around the world.

WANT TO KNOW HOW FOSSILS ARE FORMED? Turn to **page 88** to unearth some... ROCK STARS!

PREHISTORIC PUZZLES

Palaeontologists study the remains of plants and animals that lived on Earth hundreds of millions of years ago. But how do they piece together the clues – and bones – to see the full story?

BUILDING A PICTURE

Dinosaur skeletons are rarely found whole. The sediment that creates the best conditions for fossils to form was often at the bottom of rivers or seas and moved easily, so bones are usually spread widely. In fact, many sites contain fragments of bone from large numbers of different dinosaurs which must be sorted and arranged in the right positions. It's like a giant 3D jigsaw puzzle with a pile of mixed-up pieces! Here's how it's done...

1 As each piece of fossilised bone is exposed, it's coated in a special glue that stops it from crumbling and detailed notes are taken on exactly where the piece was found.

2 Then palaeontologists work out what kind of dinosaur they think the bones might have come from. They use what they know about the age of sedimentary rock to find out which dinosaurs were alive in the period of time the rock came from.

3 They also use clues from the surrounding area, such as fossils from plant and sea life. Knowing which era the bones are from helps to narrow down the list of dinosaurs they could belong to.

4 Palaeontologists look closely at every feature, from the size of the bones to the curve of the teeth and claws and compare their findings to the features of known dinosaurs.

5 Palaeontologists can use skeletons that have been found before as a kind of instruction manual or map.

6 They then begin to lay out the bones in the positions they think they might have been in when the dinosaur was alive. They look for the most intact samples, or the long bones, like those from the arms or legs, and build from there.

7 If the dinosaur is a new species, palaeontologists use images of well-known dinosaurs with similar anatomies to make informed guesses about how the bones fit together.

GUESSING GAME

In the past, when fewer fossils had been found, putting bones together to form whole skeletons took a lot of guess work. It was like trying to do a jigsaw puzzle without any idea of what the picture should look like. This is why early illustrations of dinosaurs look so different to the images we see of them today. Even when the first full Iguanodon skeletons were found in Belgium in 1878, scientists based their ideas about how to arrange the bones on the skeletons of wallabies and cassowaries.

MODERN METHODS

New technology means palaeontologists can now analyse the bones to find out how old the dinosaur they came from was when it died. They use a drill to extract a sample from the core of the bone and examine it under a microscope. Bones grow in annual spurts so they can often see age rings, like the ones you find in trees. This helps if they need to separate and sort fossils that come from different dinosaurs of the same species.

DINOSAUR PRINTS

These days, scientists can build full skeletons even if they can't find all the pieces they need. Bones can be scanned and printed on 3D printers, so if a skeleton has a missing limb, for example, a left leg could be scanned and the image flipped and printed to make a model of the right leg. Many of the full skeletons we see in museums are made this way, or by using bones from lots of different animals to make up the whole.

MARVELLOUS
Mary Anning

This pioneering palaeontologist was a woman who excelled in her field, but she was never properly acknowledged for her fantastic fossil finds. This is Mary Anning's amazing story...

DAYS GONE BY

Today, if a person stumbled upon an outstanding find, something of scientific importance that had never been seen before, you'd expect there to be a great fanfare and the discoverer's name to start trending online. That's because incredible fossil finds are huge news!

However, almost 200 years ago, when a 12-year-old girl unearthed a fossilised skull of a dinosaur in Dorset, no one really paid much attention.

MEET MARY

Mary Anning was from a poor family, didn't have a formal school education and, of course, was female, so sceptics suspected that her fossils were fake.

Even when she later made more amazing discoveries, Mary didn't receive the recognition she deserved. She was consulted by male scholars, but never allowed to participate in the Geological Society's discussions. In fact, it wasn't until 163 years after her death that she was recognised by The Royal Society as one of the 10

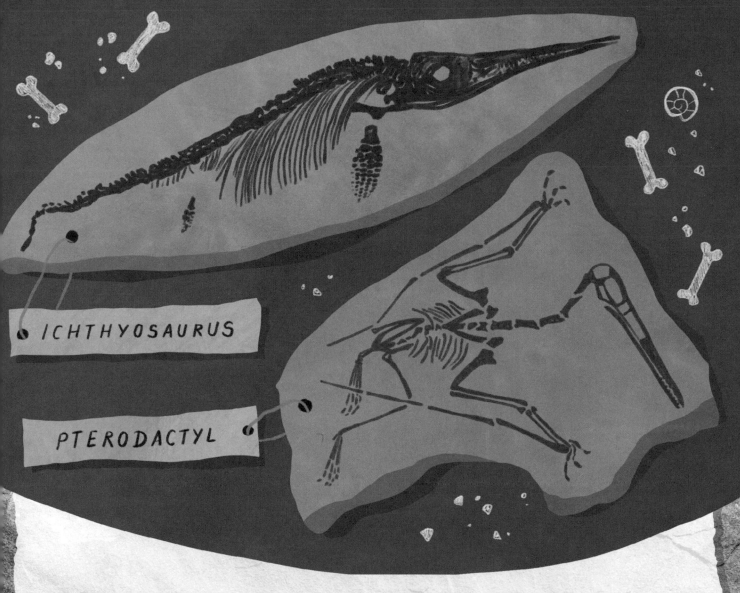

ICHTHYOSAURUS

PTERODACTYL

most influential women scientists in British history.

Born on 21 May, 1799, Mary grew up in Lyme Regis, a seaside town in southwest England. Her father Richard was a cabinetmaker but didn't earn much money, so he also sold unusual curiosities that he found on the beaches nearby.

These curios were in fact fossils, the preserved remains of plants and creatures that lived along Dorset's coast about 200 million years ago, during the Jurassic period. Today, we call it the Jurassic Coast.

Often, after a storm, when cliffs crumbled to reveal traces of ancient life, Mary and her older brother Joseph would join their dad to search for spiral-shaped ammonites that were once squid-like organisms.

However, in 1810, Mr Anning died suddenly. Worried about how the family would survive without an income, Mary continued fossil hunting and, at the age of 12,

made her first remarkable find. When her brother Joseph discovered a fossilised skull, Mary returned to the site, where she painstakingly dug for months to reveal a complete skeleton more than 5 metres long!

It was 1811, 48 years before English naturalist Charles Darwin would publish his theory of evolution by natural selection, so people weren't clued up about the extinction of certain species – the word 'dinosaur' didn't even exist until 1842.

As a result, those who looked at the skeleton wrongly believed that it was a crocodile, unaware that the mysterious creature was actually a 195-million-year-old Ichthyosaurus. Doh!

BLINDED BY SCIENCE
More discoveries followed. In 1823, Mary unearthed the complete skeleton of a long-necked Plesiosaurus,

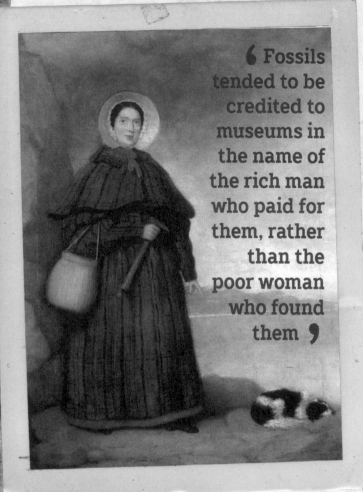

> **❝ Fossils tended to be credited to museums in the name of the rich man who paid for them, rather than the poor woman who found them ❞**

a prehistoric sea creature. Then, in 1828, she found a pterosaur, the remains of what she described as a large flying dragon, which was later named a Pterodactyl.

Mary had taught herself anatomy and geology and at first scientists and collectors were unconvinced of her expertise, but it was becoming hard to ignore the fossil hunter's growing reputation for finding and identifying ancient remains.

That said, while male masterminds wrote about Mary's groundbreaking Ichthyosaurus find in academic papers, she was not always credited. The Geological Society organised meetings to discuss her work, but the board of professionals would not let her attend because women were banned.

David Tucker, director of Lyme Regis Museum, says that if Mary had been born in 1970, she'd be heading up a university palaeontology department: 'But she was a commercial fossil hunter – she had to sell what she found. Therefore, the fossils tended to be credited to museums in the name of the rich man who paid for them, rather than the poor woman who found them.'

Despite later being given an annual payment by the British Association for the Advancement of Science, Mary Anning lived most of her life in hardship. Her death in 1847, at the age of just 47, was recorded by the Geological Society, but the fellowship still didn't admit women until 1904. Today, she's rightfully remembered as an icon of UK palaeontology.

▶ Mary Anning's plesiosaur can be seen in the Fossil Way Gallery at the Natural History Museum in London

Tray, the dog

THE LiFE OF MARY

Her parents believed she was a miracle

A woman who was holding baby Mary during a rainstorm was struck by lightning and killed. Before the incident, Mary was often sick, and afterwards she enjoyed good health. Her father Richard and her mother Mary claimed the lightning was responsible for their daughter's intelligence and determination.

She had many narrow escapes.

Landslides were (and still are) a common occurrence along the Jurassic coastline and Mary diced with death several times, dodging sudden rockfalls. Sadly, on one occasion, her dog Tray wasn't as quick to run to safety. In the famous portrait of Mary (top left), now on display at the Natural History Museum, Tray can be seen curled up sleeping at the fossil hunter's feet.

She sold her first famous fossil for £23.

The fossilised marine reptile that Mary discovered when she was 12 was bought by a local landowner for £23 and later sold at auction to the British Museum. Today at the Natural History Museum, where the Ichthyosaurus is on display, new Anning Rooms were recently opened for museum members and patrons.

Her home is now recognised by UNESCO.

The Jurassic Coast in Dorset and East Devon, which stretches for approximately 95 miles, is England's only natural UNESCO World Heritage Site and world-famous for its fossils. In January 2021, however, a dinosaur footprint was discovered on a beach in South Wales by a four-year-old girl named Lily Wilder. Experts say it's around 222 million years old.

Mary Anning's first fossil find

ROCK STARS

Everything we know about dinosaurs comes from the study of fossils – but what are they exactly?

Fossils are the preserved remains of living creatures or plants that lived on Earth millions of years ago. But they're not just old skeletons – they're bones and signs of life that have turned to stone. Preserved claws, bones and teeth are known as body fossils. Footprints, markings and imprints of scales, feathers or dinosaur skin are called trace fossils. Let's find out how they're made...

HOW ARE FOSSILS FORMED?

1 When an animal dies, the soft parts of its body begin to decay, leaving behind a skeleton – a collection of its bones.

2 It's rare for living things to become fossilised as a creature's body usually just decomposes and rots away. However, sometimes the skeleton or outer shell becomes buried in sediment, such as mud or sand. This protects it from the oxygen and bacteria that would normally make it crumble to dust.

3 Bones are made up of living parts and non-living parts. The living parts, like blood cells, fat and a protein called collagen, break down after an animal dies. The non-living parts are made from a mineral called calcium, which lasts much longer.

Water seeps into the tiny spaces where the living parts of the bone used to be. Water is full of minerals and it leaves traces of these behind – they strengthen the fragile structure of the bones, turning them into stone. It's a bit like soaking a sponge in plaster and watching it set.

4 Over thousands or even millions of years, the weight of new layers of sediment puts so much pressure on the layers below that they turn into sedimentary rock, trapping the preserved remains inside.

5 Sometimes water seeping down through the ground dissolves the buried bone or shell, leaving behind a hole exactly the same shape. Then, when waters rich in minerals like calcium fill this space, crystals can form and create a fossil in the shape of the original remains.

6 As centuries pass and seafloors and cliffs move and erode, the rocks get worn away by the weather and waves. The fossil is revealed – it's then just waiting to be discovered!

THREE FANTASTIC FOSSILS

1 DEATH-MATCH DUO

DISCOVERED Gobi desert, Mongolia, 1971
AGE 74 million years

A Velociraptor and Protoceratops were preserved in the middle of a fight! Their remains show that the Velociraptor had clawed its rival in the neck, but the Protoceratops had bitten back, breaking the predator's arm. Experts think they either fought to the death and were later covered by a sandstorm or were buried mid-battle by a sudden landslide. It's always been a wild world!

2 FISH SUPPER

DISCOVERED Solnhofen, Germany, 2009
AGE 155 million years

A pterosaur flying low over the water caught a small fish in its beak, but before it could swallow, it was attacked by the bigger, shield-snouted fish Aspidorhynchus. All three sank to the bottom of the lagoon, where their struggle was preserved forever...

VOLKER GRIENER / THE STATE MUSEUM OF NATURAL HISTORY

3 SLEEPING GIANT

DISCOVERED Alberta, Canada, 2011
AGE 110 million years

A nodosaur was swept out to sea by a flooded river and sank to the seabed where its whole body was petrified – forming a fossil that looks like a living dinosaur having a nap. This type of fossilisation happens when not only the bones but the soft body parts, such as the skin and body armour, are preserved as well.

COULD DINOSAURS WALK AGAIN?

In *Jurassic Park*, scientists bring dinosaurs back from the dead using a DNA-filled mosquito. Could that really happen? Let's find out...

A dragonfly embedded in amber

STUMBLING BLOCK #1
FINDING A FOSSIL WITH DINO DNA

In *Jurassic Park*, scientists extract dino DNA from the blood of a mosquito that's been embalmed in amber for millions of years. Is that even possible?

Amber is the hardened resin from ancient pine trees. Designed to protect trees against insects and fungi, creepy crawlies are easily trapped in the sticky substance. Shut off from oxygen by layers of sediment, the resin gradually dries out and hardens overs millions of years to form the gemstone amber – but just how likely is it to find dino DNA inside a mosquito?

Well, scientists have already found flies and mosquitoes from the time of the dinosaurs in amber. But it's rare for soft tissues like blood vessels to survive fossilisation. And even though blood has been found inside some ancient insects, it doesn't mean it will contain DNA, which breaks down quickly. In fact, the oldest DNA found so far is around a million years old. Dino DNA would be 66 times older! Do you think we'll ever find it?

DID YOU *know?*

The *Jurassic Park* series started all the way back in 1993, and its idea that all dinosaurs were scaly is pretty ancient. Since then, scientists have discovered that many dinosaurs had feathers or fur to keep them warm.

STUMBLING BLOCK #2

MAKING A DINOSAUR

Finding dino DNA can't be completely ruled out, so let's suppose scientists strike it lucky. Then what?

The reason DNA is so important is it contains all the genetic instructions that a living thing needs to grow and function. When ancient DNA is harvested from fossils, however, it's often incomplete. This can make it tricky to assemble a whole animal. It's a bit like opening a jigsaw puzzle of 5,000 pieces to find a couple of corners and the middle.

Jurassic Park's answer to this was to fill in the gaps with frog DNA. A better idea might have been to use bird DNA, as birds are dinosaurs. Incredibly, scientists are already working on a similar project. Mammoth DNA has been found in the frozen soils of Siberia, and experts are attempting to combine these fragments of genetic code with that of living elephants. If they succeed, it could be a stepping stone to a real *Jurassic Park*.

Another possibility is a process called 'reverse engineering'. The idea involves starting with an animal like a bird and working backwards until you reach its ancient ancestors. Scientists have already modified the beak of a chicken embryo to look like the snout of its dinosaur cousins. They think a dino-chicken could be a real possibility sometime in the next 50 years.

Birds could be the secret ingredient to unlocking even more Mesozoic mysteries...

STUMBLING BLOCK #3

SHOULD WE DO IT?

There are some serious ethical questions to think about and answer before ploughing ahead with recreating extinct animals. As a society, why are we doing it? Is making things just to go in a zoo a good enough reason? How would a species that has died out naturally survive in such a different world? What would it eat? Where would it live? Who would be responsible for it? Would the time and money it would take be better spent on saving the species we have left?

As the character Dr Ian Malcolm wisely said in *Jurassic Park*...

'JUST BECAUSE YOU CAN, DOESN'T MEAN THAT YOU SHOULD'

NOWHERE TO HIDE

Scientists recently scanned a 47.7-million-year-old half-ton fossilised head of a T-rex found in the US. There wasn't much of its brain left, but the shape of the skull gave clues as to which parts were more developed than others. Unlike in *Jurassic Park*, we now know that the T-rex had excellent vision – it could have seen you even if you were standing still.

THE BIG DINO QUIZ

Read the book, then put your newfound knowledge to the test!

1 What percentage of Earth's species were wiped out at the end of the Permian period? (*Turn to p6 for a hint*)

2 When was the Cretaceous? (*Turn to p8 for a hint*)

3 What tiny dinosaur was just 40cm long? (*Turn to p10 for a hint*)

4 What are animals with a backbone called? (*Turn to p12 for a hint*)

5 What ancient continent covered 30% of Earth's surface? (*Turn to p16 for a hint*)

6 How many mass extinction events have there been in Earth's history? (*Turn to p18 for a hint*)

7 What was the largest land-dwelling bug of all time? (*Turn to p28 for a hint*)

8 What was the maximum size of dinosaur eggs? (*Turn to p32 for a hint*)

9 What is the largest known carnivorous dinosaur? (*Turn to p34 for a hint*)

10 How tall was the Dreadnoughtus? (*Turn to p42 for a hint*)

11 How many kilograms of veggies did the brachiosaurus need to eat every day? (*Turn to p46 for a hint*)

12 What ancient reptile was named after a feathered Aztec god? (*Turn to p50 for a hint*)

13 What dolphin-shaped marine reptile was almost as big as a blue whale? (*Turn to p56 for a hint*)

14 In what era did the Phorusrhacids exist? (*Turn to p58 for a hint*)

15 Which species' name means 'terrible crocodile'? (*Turn to p60 for a hint*)

16 How many teeth did the Megalodon have? (*Turn to p62 for a hint*)

17 Where has the oldest known petrified forest been discovered? (*Turn to p64 for a hint*)

18 How much did the giant short-faced bear weigh? (*Turn to p68 for a hint*)

19 What species' bones were mistaken for a human giant? (*Turn to p70 for a hint*)

20 What are the closest living relative of birds? (*Turn to p74 for a hint*)

21 What do dinosaur experts call birds? (*Turn to p76 for a hint*)

22 What is the name for the study of fossils? (*Turn to p80 for a hint*)

23 What is England's only natural UNESCO World Heritage Site? (*Turn to p86 for a hint*)

24 What two dinosaurs were preserved in a death match in a fossil? (*Turn to p88 for a hint*)

25 In *Jurassic Park*, scientists extract dino DNA from what? (*Turn to p90 for a hint*)

GLOSSARY

AGILE
When something is able to move quickly and easily.

AMMONITES
Shelled marine molluscs that became extinct around 66 million years ago.

ANATOMY
The science that looks at the structure of animal species' bodies.

AQUATIC
Something that lives in the water all or most of the time.

ASTEROID
Rocks orbiting the Sun in our solar system that sometimes crash into planets, including Earth.

BIODIVERSITY
The level of variety in animal and plant life in a particular environment.

BULBOUS
Something that is round and fat in shape.

CARNIVOROUS
When an animal only eats meat to survive.

CLIMATE
The weather conditions in a particular area over a long period of time.

CONTINENTS
Large, continuous areas of land.

DEFORESTATION
When all the trees in an area are cut down, disrupting or destroying the local ecosystem.

ECOSYSTEM
The way that living organisms and their environment interact to survive.

EMBALMED
When a dead organism is preserved and prevented from decaying.

EVOLUTION
The gradual process by which all the living things on Earth have developed from earlier species.

FOLIAGE
The leaves of trees or plants.

GEOLOGISTS
People who study the Earth's structure and the materials from which it's formed.

GLACIERS
Slowly moving masses of ice formed from compacted snow.

HERBIVOROUS
When an animal only eats plants to survive.

HUMID
A high level of water vapour in the air.

MACE
A clublike weapon with a spiked metallic head.

METABOLISM
How food is converted into energy in the body of a living thing.

METEOROLOGIST
A scientist who studies the atmosphere and the weather.

MICROBES
Microscopic organisms, like bacteria.

MICROSCOPE
A scientific instrument used for looking at very small objects, including living organisms.

MINERALS
Solid substances that occur in nature but are not living.

MUZZLE
The projecting mouth and nose of some species of animal.

PROTEIN
Compounds found in food that are necessary for survival to all living organisms, helping them to grow muscle.

SEDIMENT
The particles of matter that settle in a layer at the bottom of a liquid.

TUSKS
Long, pointed teeth that stick out of the mouths of some animal species.

QUIZ ANSWERS

1. More than 90%
2. 145–66 million years ago
3. Anchiornis
4. Vertebrates
5. Pangaea
6. 5
7. Arthropleura
8. 60cm
9. Spinosaurus
10. 26 metres
11. 400kg
12. Quetzalcoatlus
13. Ichthyosaur
14. Cenozoic era
15. Deinosuchus
16. 276
17. Catskill Mountains, New York, US
18. 1 ton
19. Mastodon
20. Crocodiles
21. Avian dinosaurs
22. Palaeontology
23. The Jurassic Coast in Dorset and East Devon
24. Velociraptor and Protoceratops
25. Mosquitoes embalmed in amber

INDEX

B

Brachiosaurus 46

C

Carnotaurus 39
Continents 8, 9, 16, 17
Crocodiles 8, 60, 61, 75

D

Diplodocus 42, 43, 48,
DNA 90, 91

E

Eggs, dinosaur 32, 33
Evolution 6, 7, 8, 9, 12,
13, 14, 15, 31, 76, 77
Extinction 9, 18, 19, 20,
21, 22, 23, 31

F

Flying creatures 8, 9, 14, 15,
50, 51, 52, 53, 54, 55, 76, 77

G

Giganotosaurus 37

I

Ichthyosaur 57

M

Megalodon 62, 63

P

Palaeontology 80, 81, 82,
83, 84, 85, 86, 87, 88, 89
Plants 64, 65, 66, 67
Plesiosaur 56
Pterodactylus 52

Q

Quetzalcoatlus 51

S

Sea creatures 26, 27, 56,
57, 62, 63, 72, 73, 74, 75
Spinosaurus 34, 43
Stegosaurus 9, 44

T

Triceratops 9, 45
Tyrannosaurus rex 9, 10,
11, 15, 35, 40, 76, 90, 91

V

Velociraptor 36

First published 2023 by Button Books, an imprint of Guild of Master Craftsman Publications Ltd, Castle Place, 166 High Street, Lewes, East Sussex, BN7 1XU, UK. Copyright in the Work © GMC Publications Ltd, 2023. ISBN 978 1 78708 149 9. Distributed by Publishers Group West in the United States. All rights reserved. No part of this publication may be reproduced, stored in a retrieval system, or transmitted in any form or by any means without the prior permission of the publisher and copyright owner. While every effort has been made to obtain permission from the copyright holders for all material used in this book, the publishers will be pleased to hear from anyone who has not been appropriately acknowledged and to make the correction in future reprints. The publishers and authors can accept no legal responsibility for any consequences arising from the application of information, advice, or instructions given in this publication. A catalogue record for this book is available from the British Library. Editorial: Susie Duff, Nick Pierce, Lauren Jarvis, Sam Taylor, Chloe Rhodes, Anne Guillot, Lorna Cowan, Vincent Vincent. Design: Tim Lambert, Jo Chapman, Emily Hurlock. Publisher: Jonathan Grogan. Production: Jim Bulley. Photos/illustrations: Michelle Urra, Sara Thielker, American Museum of Natural History, Shutterstock.com, StockTrek Images, Science Photo Library. Colour origination by GMC Reprographics. Printed and bound in China.